SO-AIE-165

Cabrini College Library

Radnor, Pa.

# GREEN HILLS *of* MAGIC

# GREEN HILLS *of* MAGIC

## *WEST VIRGINIA FOLKTALES FROM EUROPE*

BY *Ruth Ann Musick*

*with illustrations by Archie L. Musick*

The University Press of Kentucky

Lexington 1970

#72090
GR
110
.W4
M78
1978

Standard Book Number 8131-1191-9
Library of Congress Catalog Card Number 79-80090

COPYRIGHT © 1970 BY THE UNIVERSITY PRESS OF KENTUCKY

A statewide cooperative scholarly publishing agency serving Berea College,
Centre College of Kentucky, Eastern Kentucky University, Kentucky State
College, Morehead State University, Murray State University, University
of Kentucky, University of Louisville, and Western Kentucky University.
*Editorial and Sales Offices: Lexington, Kentucky 40506*

To Stith Thompson and Vance Randolph,
*who have given so much of their lives*
*to the folktale and to regional folklore,*
*respectively, and to the miners*
*without whom there would have*
*been no book*

Cabrini College Library
48359
Radnor, Pa.

# Contents

## 4. Evil Spirits, Curses, and Witchcraft

## 5. Dragons, Giants, and Other Monsters

## 6. Magic Objects, Elements, and Powers

## 7. Little People

# Introduction

I FIRST SAW the hills over thirty years ago in early summer, enroute to New York City by train. The outside scenery from St. Louis had been mostly rivers and trees—and nothing could be much more intriguing—*except* green hills by the hundreds. They had appeared from nowhere, while I was asleep. I looked out one morning, and there they were—hills upon hills—billowing up like waves from a sea of moss-green velvet. *Something* had happened. We were in another world—a world of magic! Someone said it was West Virginia. All I knew was I was under a complete spell. I had never seen anything like the grandeur of these hills. There was something mystical about it all —something supernatural. A halo of soft light seemed to hover over the tops of these towering giants. It occurred to me that possibly there had been an accident, and I was in the life beyond. In any case, it was a land of magic—and myriads of green hills.

Although, at the time, I had no idea that I would ever be doing it, in the fall of 1946 I came to Fairmont State College to teach and have been here ever since. Stranger still, as I discovered later on, there actually *was* magic in the hills—tales of magic, brought over from Europe or Asia Minor by the men who came to work in the West Virginia coal mines.

Those who have lived in this region, or have read much about it, know that in and around these hills and mountains are mines, and the mines bring in the chief income of the state. Consequently, there are hundreds of miners in West Virginia, many of whom remember and tell tales of fantastic splendor which they heard when they were children.

Some people may think it strange that only the miners and their families tell tales of magic—and almost no one else—but I'm not so sure. It may be that all this has something to do with the miners themselves. In the early 1900s, when the coal-mine boom of this country beckoned to immigrants from Europe, men and boys came from almost every country and from various walks of life. Some were miners in Europe, some were peasants or farmers, some had a trade, but all of them were poor. And they were all dreamers, who dreamed of a better life for themselves and their families; in many cases their dreams were realized, although at first they had to work for almost nothing, and life was hard.

The work of the miners, even in times of prosperity, may have something to do with their love of wonder and magic. Theirs is a life of contrast and uncertainty.

The typical mining town in West Virginia has its river, along which runs a railroad track, connecting with the mines. Much of the time slow-moving cars loaded with coal come in from the mine, and empty cars go back, with a kind of around-the-clock regularity. Coal is transported also by barge on one of the many rivers. The actual labor, down in the mines, is usually a fixed routine. Each man has a particular job—usually two men work together—which he does so many hours a day, with little variation except in times of strike or calamity.

But there *are* strikes and there *are* calamities. Sometimes no one knows the real cause of a mine tragedy; sometimes the cause is known, but nothing can be done about it. From time to time there are explosions, accidents, sudden gas, slate falls, and cave-ins that kill or pen-in miners so that they cannot be rescued. All this may happen at any time in the best of mines.

Perhaps all this uncertainty keeps alive the stories these men heard when they were children. Perhaps to them these stories are a kind of escape from the dark uncertainty of the underground and the fear of sudden death or tragedy.

Even so, it is the miners and their families who know these stories and tell them with childlike enthusiasm, so that the listener is transported to another world. And, in a land where the art of oral taletelling is almost a thing of the past, this is a rare experience.

Many of these tales were told by the miners themselves —sometimes in the original languages—and recorded on tape by me. Others were told by miners or miners' families to students (often younger relatives) and brought in as themes or as parts of their folklore collections. Still others were written up by the miners and sent in by mail or brought in by students. Except for correcting grammatical errors, deleting repetitious and extraneous matter, and transferring explanatory material to the notes, I have set down these tales as I received them.

Ordinarily, I suppose, when one thinks of miners, he thinks of heavy drinkers and rough men. Perhaps in many cases this is true. I am confident, however, that the older people who gave so generously of their time to make recordings for me—or who told stories orally or who wrote them and sent them in—undoubtedly had certain sensitive qualities and dreamed of spendid and fantastic lives. Otherwise, how could they have kept these tales of wonder and magic alive all these years?

Transcribing these stories is difficult. I have recorded

tales with paper and pencil, by tape recorder, and through friends and students who know the native language of the storyteller. Generally speaking, none of these methods is satisfactory. The lack of knowledge of English on the part of the speaker and my deficiency in foreign languages are the chief problems. If the storyteller speaks in his native tongue—unless I have an unusually good translator—the meaning may be changed. On the other hand, if I record or set down the story in broken English, it is sometimes extremely hard to know exactly what is meant. However, by checking and rechecking the tapes with the teller and translator, and by a minimum correction of grammatical and idiomatic errors, I believe these stories are much as the tellers intended them to be.

In classifying the tales, a number of methods could have been used, including listing them according to countries or contributors, or by following the Aarne-Thompson classification suggested in *The Types of the Folk-Tale*, or by dividing them into märchen and other types, or as I did. I chose the following classification because it seemed to be the best one for these particular stories, everything considered.

For anyone interested, notes about the contributors (including brief biographies of some of the people who contributed a number of stories) and comparisons to similar stories in other collections are given at the end of the book.

# Acknowledgments

SOME OF THE stories in this collection were previously published in *The Telltale Lilac Bush and Other West Virginia Ghost Tales* (Lexington: University of Kentucky Press, 1965), in *Midwest Folklore*, and in *West Virginia Folklore*. I wish to thank the publishers involved for permission to use the material again.

Also, I wish to thank all the contributors of stories. Many of the older taletellers spoke no English, and so their stories had to be translated, and in many cases I believe the results are better than when told in broken English. I especially want to thank those who contributed a number of stories, including John Novak (Polish), Joe Catania (Italian, Sicily), Arpad Puskas (Hungarian), Rocco Pantalone (Italian), Frank Pazdric (Austrian), Ali Ishmael (Turkish), Grace Hervatin (Italian), Macrina Fernandez Garcia and her daughter, Anita Garcia Alvarez (Spanish), and all the others, including my students and friends who have helped in any way.

In addition, I would like to thank Professor Stith Thompson, without whose books, *The Folktale*, *Motif Index of Folk Literature* (1955-1958), and the Aarne-Thompson *Types of the Folktale* (1961), it would be impossible to classify any of these tales; Vance Randolph, whose excellent collections have been an inspiration and guide to me for years; and Professor William Hugh Jansen, who gave so generously of his time in making many helpful suggestions in the publication of *Lilac Bush* and has given further suggestions for this book.

Besides these, I would also like to thank Mrs. Logan Carroll (Elinor Watson Carroll), whose great-grandfather was one of the early coal kings of the area and whose information concerning early Marion County mining days and other matters has been extremely helpful.

And, last, I want to thank my brother, Archie L. Musick, who made the illustrations for this book, all of which I think add immeasurably in emphasizing some of the unique situations depicted in the tales.

R. A. M.
*Fairmont*
*March 9, 1969*

Man against
the Devil

# 1. The Legend of Twardowski

To THIS DAY people in Poland speak of the legendary figure
of Twardowski with awe, and repeat tales of his wondrous
travels and doings while on earth, as of no one else. If a
man lives to a very venerable age or past the century mark,
he is said to be as old as Twardowski. Or, if a man has
unusual physical strength, he is said to be as strong as
Twardowski. Or, if he is unusually bright and cunning,
he is said to be as clever as Twardowski. Children who
hear the legend of Twardowski diligently aspire to that
character's great and varied powers.

1

Twardowski was a God-fearing lad of seventeen years, when a great change came about in his life. He was an orphan and did not remember his parents. He was brought up by a man and wife who were good people, but he never seemed to do enough to please them. When the wife died, the master became mean, miserly, and so exacting that it was impossible to please him in anything. Finally Twardowski lost all patience at a torrent of his master's abusive words, and he went out of the house muttering to himself, "I would rather work for the devil than this man!"

No sooner had he spoken the words, than before him stood a man in fine dress and tall silk hat, bespeaking a man of the world—and leisure.

"I heard your words, my lad. I shall be very glad to relieve you of this burdensome place if you will come with me."

Twardowski looked at the friendly man and his fine dress. Then he happened to look at the stranger's feet and saw that they were not shod in shoes but were cloven hoofs. "Ah, ha!" he thought to himself. "So this is the kind of fine gentleman he is!" A sense of adventure seized him, and he was as one possessed to know more. Then, since he felt that he had done his duty by his master, he was free to go.

"Very well," he said to the devil, "what can you offer me better than I have here?"

"It will be better, I promise you," the devil said with a sly smile. "You said you would rather work for me than for your master, so you cannot go back on your word."

Twardowski could still hear his master ranting and raving, so he said, "Very well, I shall go."

No sooner had he said the words than he was caught up in a rush of whirlwind, and before he could catch his breath again, he found himself in a region of smoke and flames, terrible to behold. He looked about him and saw huge black cauldrons higher than his head, steaming and boiling. Spine-chilling wails—a continual sound of moaning and lamenting—filled the air. To an iron pillar was chained a miserable creature, emaciated and hollow-eyed.

"And who is that?" Twardowski asked.

The devil smiled and said, "Oh, that is Judas Iscariot. It will be your job to flail him five hundred times a day."

"That will be a pleasure," said Twardowski.

"And you must keep up the fire under these cauldrons. Here are a pair of iron shoes you can put on so that the fires won't burn your feet. When you wear these out you can demand your pay and go back to earth."

Twardowski was glad to change into the iron shoes, because the bottoms of his feet were already burning. But the minute he put them on, he knew that he would never be able to get them off again and that the devil had outwitted him. It would be hard to go far in those heavy iron shoes.

"And what will be my pay for my service?" he asked.

Again the devil smiled and said, "When and if you are clever enough to get away from here you may take some souls out of purgatory for your pay. However, in any case you cannot go away from here until you have worn holes in the bottom of those iron shoes, so we will not have to worry about that for a long time. Now, unless you want to become chained to an iron pillar like Iscariot, you had better do as I tell you, and as long as you serve me well, I shall treat you kindly. Now, Iscariot has not had his five hundred lashes today, so while I go out into the world and look for more souls, you can do what I have outlined for you."

3

Twardowski looked about him. He saw many wretches shod in iron shoes, chopping wood and replenishing the great, bubbling cauldrons of souls. But he thought to himself, "I may be here, but I shall not be here long. I have been outwitted once, but never again. I shall not become such as these poor wretches."

He picked up the great iron flail to give Iscariot his five hundred lashes. Iscariot fell on his knees and begged him not to whip him. "You are a good man. Spare me once, I beg of you. All these long years, I have been getting five hundred lashes a day. Do you not think I have paid enough for my sins?"

Twardowski had a kind heart, and so even this wretch who had committed the worst of sins by betraying Christ, stayed his hand. "I shall never be able to get away from here if I don't do what I'm told to do."

"If you will spare me the lashes only once, I shall tell you a secret. I can help free you quickly, for the devil is a man of his word."

"Very well," Twardowski agreed. "I am in no mood to give anyone five hundred lashes today. What is the secret?"

"You are a good man. You are the first one—the first one to spare me. Now perhaps I shall go to my rest at last, for the devil said if and when I met a man who had the heart not to whip me, he would let me go to my peaceful rest. Come, quickly. My nails are like rasps. I shall scratch holes in the bottoms of your shoes."

And it didn't take him long to do it—much to Twardowski's surprise. His feet burned through the holes in the bottoms, but he didn't mind. He awaited the devil's return. He dared not lie down, for the ground was hot —like the top of a brick stove. Sweat poured down his face and body, and there was no water to drink. He tried

to replenish the fires under the cauldrons of moaning souls, but the sound of suffering stayed his hand. His cruel master now seemed like an angel in comparison to what confronted him here. He spread his sheepskin coat on the hot ground and went to sleep.

He had no more than closed his eyes when, with a terrible rush of wind, the devil was there again, ranting and raving.

"What is the meaning of this? I leave you to replenish the fires and you sleep! Is this the way you work?" Then he looked around and saw Iscariot slumped in peaceful, eternal sleep, and his anger became even greater. "So you have outwitted me!"

"This work is not to my liking," Twardowski said calmly. "See, I have holes in the bottoms of my shoes. You said that you would set me free and give me my pay when I had them."

Then the devil tore his hair, his clothes, and was so angry that sparks flew from his hoofs and flames from his mouth, but Twardowski remained calm and unafraid, and waited for the devil to contain himself.

When the devil had exhausted his temper, he said, "Very well. You are not the man I want here. You do not co-operate."

Twardowski held out one foot and then the other, while the devil cut the iron chain that held the shoes on his feet.

"Now, out of my sight!" the devil fumed. "Take your souls and go—but remember I shall follow you. And the day will come when I shall get the best of you and bring you back. And then, you shall see what I can do to make you pay for this!"

Twardowski hopped around on the hot ground in his bare feet, grabbed his sheep-lined jacket, reached up into the high cauldron, and stirred it among the souls. To every hair in the coat, a soul clung and was taken out. One mother grabbed a hair, and her daughter grabbed the mother by the feet and was lifted out also. Twardowski had quite a load, but he flung it over his shoulder, and the devil struck the ground with his hoofs, and that terrible rush of wind came and carried Twardowski and his load of souls away from there. He found himself on earth again, and, it being night, he lay down to sleep.

In the morning when he awoke, he found himself on a glorious mountaintop with a beautiful meadow. There before him was a wondrous sight—a great herd of sheep. He looked at his sheep-lined coat and saw that it was clean of souls. They had all disappeared. "Well, what better could they now be than sheep?" he thought. With that he said his morning devotions, found a spring and washed his face and hands, and was wondering what next, when before him appeared the radiant figure of the Virgin Mary. She spoke in a beautiful voice, but it sounded more as an echo than direct speech. "Twardowski, sell me your great flock of sheep."

Twardowski bowed and said, "It is beneath the dignity of so gracious a lady to bargain with a common man, such as I."

Immediately she disappeared and a masculine figure appeared, dressed in robes of Biblical times. "Twardowski," He began.

"How is it that you know my name, since I am a stranger here?"

The face before him lighted up with a smile and He said, "I know."

"I think You do know, my Lord," Twardowski agreed respectfully and with awe. "You have come for the sheep?"

"What riches can I give you for all those sheep, Twardowski?"

Twardowski thought a moment and said, "A staff that will help me in times of trouble and will do my bidding, and a bag that I can carry with me wherever I go, and if the Lord would be so gracious—let me live as long as I desire."

"You are a good lad, Twardowski. Your wish shall be granted and here are your staff and bag—a bag big enough to carry a man. So long as you live according to God's will, all will go well for you." Then the figure and the sheep disappeared.

Twardowski took the staff and the bag and started out. As he went down the mountainside, he came upon some poor peasants who were crying. He asked them what was the matter. At first they were afraid of him, but since he was so young and fine-looking, they gained courage and told him of Myda and his terrible gang of brigands in the mountains far away, who came to the villages and plundered and took away their sheep and cattle, and killed the men who resisted them.

"Well, well," said Twardowski, "I shall look into this and see what I can do about it."

"He has killed so many people," continued the peasant, "that if one had a staff like yours for every person, it would make a stack of staffs as high as yours and as great in breadth and depth. It is said that he has killed even his own mother and father."

They gave Twardowski some bread and cheese and he started out in the direction from whence the robbers were known to come. For days he traveled and slept by night. Finally when he came to a high mountain and approached

8

the entrance of a cave, he heard loud drunken laughter, singing and boisterousness. There was a smell of wood smoke and roast meat.

When the brigands saw him, they fell upon him, took his cane and bag, and marched him to their cruel captain. They were all for killing him.

"If you kill me, my staff will kill you," Twardowski told them. Then with a quick wrench and twist, he was out of their grasp, grabbed his staff and bag, and said, "Staff, beat these brigands, so that they will know what a licking really is."

With that the staff jumped out of his hand and danced over the heads of the brigands, beating them so that they scattered and ran for their lives. Twardowski looked at the captain, who was laughing at his silly henchmen who ran from such a little thing as a staff.

"Why do you laugh?" Twardowski asked.

While Twardowski's back was turned the henchmen returned and grabbed the bag that he carried, thinking he had gold in it, since it seemed so full and heavy. Twardowski turned and saw the henchmen about to open the bag and cried, "Don't open it! It is full of the devil's imps." Again the robbers laughed. "If you do not believe me," Twardowski said, "I shall lay this bag down, and if you take sticks and beat it, you will hear. . . ."

"Why do you carry the devil's imps?" asked the captain of the robbers.

"So that they won't torment me and lead me astray."

Several of the robbers took huge sticks and beat the bag, and great crying and moaning and begging came from the bag. Finally, when it seemed that all would be pulp, Twardowski stayed the whipping and opened the bag, out of which jumped creatures with long tails, hoofed feet, and tiny horns on their heads, who, screaming, ran for their lives out of the cave.

The robbers were terrified and amazed. Twardowski had told the truth. They decided to humor him until he fell asleep and then burn his staff and kill him. They fed Twardowski and told tales of their horrible adventures, and asked him to join their band. Twardowski thanked them for their invitation, but told them he was tired and would go to sleep. He had almost dozed off when the robbers took his staff and threw it on the fire. But it cried out with a loud voice, "Twardowski, save me, save me!"

Twardowski woke up and commanded the staff to beat the robbers again so that they would beg for mercy. Again the staff jumped about, beating and tripping the robbers until they ran away. Even the captain fled for his life, thinking this some sorcery or black magic.

When the robbers had fled, Twardowski lay down and went to sleep, commanding the staff to guard him. In the morning he rounded up the herd of cattle, packed the sacks of grain and money on their backs, and returned them to the village. The villagers were so grateful when they saw their goods and cattle being returned that they lifted Twardowski on their shoulders and carried him about, singing for joy. They made a great festival on that day, dancing all day and all night. Several elders from the village told Twardowski he could choose the prettiest girl for his bride, but he thanked them for their kind offer, saying that he was a wanderer and had much of the world yet, to see, so he was not ready to settle down.

Thus began the legend that grew with the years, as Twardowski went about doing deeds of kindness and helping the poor and needy. Years went by as quickly as if one were sifting peas through his fingers. One day he came upon an aged father, weeping.

"Why do you cry?" Twardowski asked.

"The devil is to take my son," the old man said.

"How can that be so?" Twardowski asked.

Then the old man told Twardowski a fantastic tale. Long ago when he was returning from a long journey, his team of horses got stuck in a bog, and, try as he would, he could not get them out. Finally when he despaired of saving his horses, a well-dressed figure appeared before him and said, "What will you give me if I help you?"

"Anything. Anything I have," the man promised, and then he noticed that the well-dressed stranger had hoofs for feet, but he was so desperate that he didn't care—just so he didn't lose his valuable horses. He had a good hundred miles to get home and it was impossible to walk.

"Very well," said the stranger. "I want that which you have, but which you do not yet know you have. You do not have it with you, but I shall come for it in good time."

The man helped him get his horses out with such ease that it seemed simple. He invited the stranger to come with him, but he refused and said he would come and collect his pay later.

The old man now continued. "I thought he was just joking, but I should have known better. He asked me to sign a paper to the effect that seventeen years from that time he might come for his pay—and I was not to be grudging, but give it to him. It seemed simple, but now I know what scheme he had in mind, for when I reached home I found that my wife had given birth to a son, and was so happy about it, I forgot the devil—for that is who it was—and gave it no more thought. As my son grew, he showed an inclination to study for the priesthood, so I let

11

him. Yesterday he was seventeen, and a messenger has arrived with a note that a debt of seventeen years' standing is to be collected. He demands services of my son in payment. What can I do? What can I do—I cannot let my son pay for my grievous ignorance and sin!"

Twardowski thought a moment and said, "Let your son go, but first tell him when he gets to Hades to tell the devil that he can do no work except that of building a church. He will be a better priest for having seen that place—and what it's like."

The father conveyed the message to his son and told him to go with the messenger, praying all the while that Twardowski was right.

The son went as he was told to do. When he arrived in Hades, the devil immediately ordered him to keep the great cauldrons of souls boiling at full heat. The son only shook his head and said, "I cannot do that. I have come here to build a church, and that is what I shall do, so that these poor souls can pray and redeem themselves."

The devil became so angry he turned a glowing red, like a live coal, from head to foot. He clicked his hoofs together so viciously that sparks flew, grabbed the contract that the father had signed seventeen years earlier, and threw it at the young man, saying, "Get out of my sight! A church he wants to build here! The word is never to be uttered here even—and he wants to build a church!"

The son grabbed the contract and ran for his life, but on his way home he got lost and could not find his way back, so that he wandered about for years and years.

Years later, when he became a priest, he had a parish in the mountains. The captain of the robbers, now an aged man, came and told him that he had sinned greatly and that now he wished to make amends. As a penance, the priest gave him his cane and told him to stick it in the ground and carry water to it by mouth, until the tree took root, grew, and bore fruit. The brigand did so, carrying water in his mouth to water the tree every day, until the dry stick began to bud and leaf out and flourish. Years later, when the tree was full of fruit, he went to the priest and hold him that the tree was now full of apples. The priest told him he would hear his confession. And as the robber confessed his sins, for each sin, an apple fell from the tree. Finally there were only two apples left on the tree.

"And what sins are those?" asked the priest.

Finally the aged robber confessed that they were his mother and father whom he had killed. When he had confessed this, the apples fell, the priest gave him absolution, and told him he would now rest in peace. The robber died and the priest buried him under the apple tree.

Twardowski had lived a long time and Lady Death had long yearned to gather him to her bosom. So she finally got permission from God to go and find Twardowski but could take him *only* if he were willing. At that time Death was a beautiful lady, full-fleshed and rosy cheeked, with eyes like pools in a forest, and a winning smile.

When she found Twardowski she told him she had come for him and he must come with her. He told her that he was not ready to go with her yet, but if she were willing to follow him about he would think about it and make up his mind. Days went by and then weeks, and Lady Death became tired of keeping up with him.

"If you are tired, get in this bag and I shall carry you," Twardowski told her.

She was so weary that she was glad to be carried. But she was a load and was too close for comfort, so Twardowski

13

hung the bag in a tree in the forest and told her that he would return soon. However, one adventure after another came along, keeping him away for a good many months, so that when he did return, he found her emaciated beyond recognition—so emaciated that she was nothing but skin and bones. She was so angry at him that she told him that she would never take him; that he would never die; that he would have to wander the earth unto eternity for doing this terrible thing to her.

When she returned to God and told Him all that had happened, He told her that she would no longer be beautiful and enticing, but would have to remain thus—emaciated and blind, wandering the earth—no more to do her own choosing, but blundering and taking only those who were fortunate enough to fall near her hand.

All the years that Twardowski was wandering about and doing good, the devil and his imps were keeping close watch on him, trying their best to tempt him away from his godly ways of doing good in the world. Now that Twardowski was getting old and feeble, it would be easier to get the best of him. Thus they waylaid him one day and tied him up.

"We shall build a mill and grind him slowly to make him suffer for all the suffering he has caused us," said the devil to his imps. "But we must build quickly, for we must get it done by midnight or when the cock crows, or all will be lost."

But, just as they were putting the last stone into place, the cock crowed and the midnight hour struck. So their labor fell apart, and Twardowski with one heave pulled himself free again. Again the devil was so angry at being outwitted that he struck his hoofs together until the sparks flew, and where his hoofs struck the rock, the marks can still be seen this day. To this day, it is called Twardowski's rock with the devil's prints.

True, Twardowski was getting feeble and tired. It seemed that Death would be a good friend to have now. But he knew that he would never have the privilege of rest as others knew it, for Death had sworn never to take him away. The devil's imps were dancing with joy at his feebleness; they would get him yet. Finally, one day he told them that they could carry him; as they did so, he asked them to stop so he could sing his prayers. He did this so often that the imps wearied of his singing and the resting, for they felt that they would never get him where they wanted him, so they finally said in disgust, "You can just stay here. We don't want you if all you can do is sing prayers. We don't stay around people who says prayers and think only of God. You no longer interest us." And they went away, leaving him—a thin, frail man—to say his prayers alone.

Finally a spider took pity on Twardowski and wove a long web and tied it to him securely; then she unwound her web and let the wind blow him into the air. And the wind caught up the web and lifted Twardowski up and up and up and up—till, since the spider kept spinning her web, he finally reached the moon. And that is the face you see when the moon is big and bright. So that now, people in Poland say that Twardowski is neither on earth or in heaven —but up there in the moon.

## 2. The Man Who Sold His Shadow

ONCE IN FAR-OFF Ireland there was a man named John O'Hara, who had been having bad luck for a long time. He had lost his job; his wife had taken ill and died; and nothing had gone right. He decided to take his own life because he had no money to pay his debts and had nothing to live for. So, on a foggy Wednesday night, he walked to the bridge crossing the river and had climbed upon the rail to jump when a voice called to him to wait; that he wanted to talk to him.

The man told John that he would make a bargain with him. He said that he would buy his shadow for all the money he would ever need. John asked how he was going to get the money, and the stranger replied that if John would agree to the terms, his purse would never be empty again. John took the stranger's word and accepted the bargain. When he was told to look in his purse, he found it was full of gold coins.

For a long time after the incident John was happy and prosperous, but eventually people began to ask questions about where he had got all his money and why he had no shadow when the sun was shining. John could not answer these questions, and since a great many robberies were taking place at the time, he was blamed for them and was sent to prison, where he died. He had willed all his money to the poor people of Ireland, who erected a statue to his memory.

# 3. Patience

A LONG TIME AGO, away up in the mountains in old Turkey, there was a buried treasure, consisting of many hundred dollars' worth of gold and silver. This money was possessed by the devil, and a certain procedure had to be followed in order to obtain it. The people in town knew about the money buried in the mountain, but were either afraid to do anything about it, or didn't know how to go about getting it.

One day a priest came along, and having heard the story he went around town to see if he could find a youth with enough patience and courage to take the course of action necessary to gain the treasure. He searched the town and finally found a man who thought he would be able to do what was needed.

The priest explained, "You must have a lot of patience, because it will take from midnight to early sunrise. You will have to be able to withstand all the things the devil will put forth to frighten you—such as appearing in the form of a ghost, a giant snake, a huge beast of some kind, or a great storm or fire—and you must not show any fear."

The man agreed and they went up the mountain. The high priest started reading out of a book that he had with him, and kept reading. Finally he explained to the youth that he should not have much clothing on and should hold a small bottle in his right hand, since after all the demonstrations were over, the devil would appear as a huge serpent and would finally get small enough to crawl up his body and down into the bottle.

The young man agreed to this and they started the routine necessary to obtain the treasure, as the priest continued to read. While he was reading, the sky turned fiery red, with flames and smoke everywhere, but the man was able to withstand this gesture of the devil. Soon after, the devil appeared as a monstrous beast. Then he caused a great thunderstorm, and many other such things, to try to frighten the youth—to see if he could break him down, make him show fear, or lose patience. All this took a long time.

It was now early in the morning, and, as the priest had explained, the devil appeared as a huge serpent, with a great mouth ready to swallow the man alive, it seemed. The priest had previously explained, "Whatever he does, do not fear him. He cannot harm you unless you break your promise—unless you become impatient or afraid and move from the scene of the treasure."

At this time all the chests of money were on top of the ground. Everything was practically over, and as the serpent approached the youth it began to get smaller and started crawling up his right leg. This took considerable time, but it finally succeeded. It crawled up to his right arm and headed down toward his right hand, where the man held the small bottle. And, as time passed, it went into the bottle, with only about one-half inch of tail sticking out, but it seemed to take hours and hours to get the rest of the tail into the bottle.

It was almost daylight by this time, and everything had to be over before the sun rose. The young man stood and stood. . . . And, as you might think, he got impatient, took his left hand, and slammed the tail into the bottle.

As he did that, the cases of money, the chests of gold and silver, all sank back into the ground, and it seemed as if heaven and earth were coming to pieces. The two men, the priest and the youth, disappeared and didn't return home for about seven years. And they didn't know what had happened to them.

## 4. "El Caballo con Alas"

ALBERTO RODRIGUEZ had a close friend named Gabriel Fernandez. Gabriel had received word that his mother, who lived in the neighboring village of Molina, was quite ill, and he wanted to go and see her. His wife was expecting their first child at any moment, however, and he felt he should be with her. Finally, at his wife's insistence, he decided to see his mother, but promised he would be home by late afternoon.

In order to reach the village of Molina, Gabriel, like all others before him, had to cross a narrow stream. There were large flat rocks, which the villagers used as stepping-stones, from one edge of the stream to the other. No one could recall a time when the water was so high that it was impossible to cross.

Gabriel reached the home of his parents and was informed that his mother was somewhat improved. He ate dinner with his father, and then helped him with the farmwork. About noon, when it had started to rain quite heavily, his mother thought he should start for home. She was afraid the stream would overflow and be impossible to cross, but the two men assured her there was no danger, since they had had many rains much heavier than this one, and the streams had never become impossible to cross by foot.

By late afternoon, Gabriel saw that his mother was feeling better and was in no danger, so he bade them goodby. His mother wanted him to stay overnight, but he insisted on leaving because he had promised his wife he would return home that day. When he reached the stream, he saw it was so swollen and the current so swift that crossing would be impossible. He stood at the edge of the stream, not knowing what to do. In desperation, he said loudly, "I would give my soul for some way to cross this stream."

At that moment he heard a noise behind him and, on turning around, saw a black horse. Thinking that it was a horse from a neighboring farm, he decided to ride it across the stream and leave it on the other side, where its owner would surely see it.

Gabriel got on the horse's back, but instead of walking across the stream, the creature seemed to sprout wings, and was *flying*. Gabriel was shocked. Then he remembered the words he had uttered, "I would give my soul for some way to cross this stream."

He felt sure that the horse was a messenger from the devil or even the devil himself. Making the sign of the cross he said, "My God, what did I say? Forgive me, I did not mean it." As he did so, the horse dropped him from its back.

In the meantime, Gabriel's wife was greatly concerned about him, for it was already nightfall. She asked Alberto's wife, who had been staying with her that day, to ask her husband if he would go and try to find him. Alberto and two other villagers took their lanterns and walked to the stream. There they found Gabriel unconscious. They carried him home and called a doctor, who found he had several broken ribs, a fractured ankle, and severe back injuries, all of which would necessitate many weeks in bed.

When he woke up, and Alberto asked what had happened, Gabriel told him the story about the black horse with wings. He could see by the expression on his friend's face that he did not believe him, and said, "You must believe me, Alberto. We have known each other since childhood. Have you ever known me to be one given to telling fancy tales or lies?"

Alberto admitted that he knew him to be a sincere and sensible man.

Gabriel said, "When the horse dropped me, I was still conscious. When I landed on the edge of the stream, the lower part of my body was in the water, and I was in such great pain that I could not move. I prayed to God to give me strength to pull myself up on the ground so that I would not drown. God must have heard my prayers, for I managed to crawl away from the water. That is all I remember until I woke up in this bed."

Alberto still found the story hard to believe, but he knew that Gabriel could not have walked across the swollen stream, and he also knew that the current was too swift for him to have swum across. Besides, he knew that his friend could not swim. So he came to the conclusion that he must believe the story. However, he said, "Gabriel, I believe you, but I advise you not to repeat this story to anyone, for they would surely think you had lost your senses. We must tell only the members of your family."

The following day, Gabriel's wife gave birth to a son,

and on his right hip was a birthmark in the shape of a horse's hoof.

Since that time at least one male member in the Fernandez family in each generation has had the same birthmark in exactly the same spot.

# *5.* General Staats and the Devil

General Jonathan Staats of Ripley, West Virginia, was a general of consequence in the Civil War, but a man not always trusted in other than military matters. One evening he sat musing at the fireside on the hardness of life in a new country and the difficulty of getting wealth, for old Jonathan was fond of money, and the lack of it distressed him worse than a conscience.

"If only I could have gold," he muttered, "I'd sell my soul for it."

Suddenly something came down the chimney. The general was dazzled by a burst of sparks, from which stepped forth a lank personage in black velvet, clean ruffles, and bright jewels.

"Talk quick, General," said the unknown, "for in fifteen minutes I must be fifteen miles away in Ravenswood." Picking up a live coal in his fingers, he looked at his watch by its light. "Come, you know me. It's a bargain?"

The general was a little slow to recover his wits, but the

word *bargain* put him on his mettle, and he began to think of advantageous terms.

"What proof is there that you can do your part in the compact?" he inquired.

The unknown ran his fingers through his hair, and a shower of guineas jingled onto the floor. They were warm, but Jonathan in his eagerness fell on his hands and knees and gathered them to his breast.

"Give me some liquor," demanded Satan, for, of course, he was no other, and filling a tankard with rum, he lighted it with a candle, remarked affably, "To our better acquaintance," and tossed off the blazing dram at a gulp. "I will make you the richest man in the state. Sign this paper and on the first day of every month I will fill your boots with gold; but if you try any tricks with me you will repent it, for I know you, Jonathan. Sign!"

Jonathan hesitated.

"Humph!" sneered his majesty. "You have put me to all this trouble for nothing!" And he began to gather up the guineas that Jonathan had placed on the table.

This was more than the victim of his wiles could stand. He seized a pen that was held out to him and trembled violently as a paper was placed before him. But when he found that his name was to appear with some of the most distinguished in the state, his nerves grew steadier and he placed his autograph among those of the eminent company.

"Good!" exclaimed the devil, and wrapping his cloak about him he stepped into the fire and was up the chimney in a twinkling.

Shrewd Jonathan went out the next day and bought the biggest pair of boots he could find in Ripley. He hung them on the crane on the last night of that and all the succeeding months so long as he lived, and on the next morning they brimmed with coins. Staats rolled in riches. The neighbors regarded his sudden wealth with amazement, then with envy, but afterward with suspicion. All the same, Jonathan was not getting rich fast enough to suit himself.

When the devil came to make one of the periodical payments, he poured guineas down the chimney for half an hour without succeeding to fill the boots. Bushel after bushel of gold he emptied into those spacious moneybags without causing an overflow; finally he descended to the fireplace to see why.

Jonathan had cut the soles from the boots, and the floor was knee-deep in money. With a grin at the general's smartness, the devil disappeared, but in a few minutes a smell of sulphur pervaded the premises, and the house burst into flames. Jonathan escaped in his shirt, and tore his hair as he saw the fire crawl serpentlike over the beams and the fantastic smoke-forms dance in the windows.

Then a thought crossed his mind and he grew calm. The gold that was hidden in the cupboard, floor, and chest would melt down in the heat and could be quarried out by the hundredweight, so that he could be well-to-do again. Before the ruins were cooled, he was delving amid the rubbish, but not an ounce of gold could be discovered. Every bit of his wealth had disappeared.

It was not long after that the general died, and to quiet some rumors of disturbance in the graveyard his coffin was dug up. It was empty.

## II

# Efforts to
# Outwit Death

## *6.* The White Bird of Death

ALONG WITH the black coach with the six fog-gray horses, the Irish tell of a great White Bird that came for the souls of children and infants that were about to die. This bird was very large and pure white. The only sound it made was with its powerful wings, and the soft noise made by the air filtering through the wing feathers while the White Bird glided around the dwelling of the sick infant or child.

This is the story of Dennis O'Neal and his grandson, Jamie.

Dennis and Jamie were the last of the O'Neals. This was because Dennis had lost his sons and brothers in a surprise raid by the Danes a year before this event took place. Jamie was the son of Paddy, who was the oldest of the O'Neals fathered by Dennis. Jamie and his mother made their home with Dennis, in the strong, fortlike house of the O'Neals.

Jamie was the pride and joy of his grandsire, and the only hope of keeping the family name of O'Neal from becoming past history. Naturally, as the only heir, he was tutored and trained so that he could grow up and assume the responsibility of being the chief in fact as well as in name.

Now Jamie had reached the age of ten and, with the training of Dennis and the old family retainer, Tim Kelly, was an able horseman, a good archer, and was learning the use of the sword and dirk. He could read, write, and do small problems in arithmetic reasonably well. Jamie was able to speak and understand French, Latin, and Welsh. He had some knowledge of astronomy that would be useful to an able horseman.

Jamie was truly a born chieftain, and his grandfather was justly proud. Dennis had visions of the name O'Neal coming into future glory to match and to surpass the glory and honor won in the past by the sons of the family of O'Neal.

Suddenly disaster struck. Jamie became the victim of some strange sickness. The doctor could do nothing to help the boy. Dennis sent to Dublin for the most learned doctor, but even this doctor was helpless. Jamie was slowly wasting away. As always in such cases, there were good people coming with suggestions and offers of help and prayer.

One day the parish priest came with a doctor from Spain. This doctor offered to do what he could for Jamie, and was taken at once to the sickroom. This doctor seemed to know what to do. He mixed his medicines and assumed the care of the sick lad, with the confidence that comes from knowledge and experience. Jamie began to show some signs of holding on. One evening the doctor told Dennis that the next forty-eight hours, would tell the tale. If Jamie could last that long, he would get well.

That night Dennis was so overwrought with worry and hope that he went out to walk in the courtyard. It was a still, calm night; not a breath of air was moving. Suddenly Dennis heard the noise of wind in the leaves, only there were no trees within his hearing range. Then he knew. It was the White Bird of Death that had come for Jamie. He rushed to his grandson's room and, closing the door, started to block off the windows to keep the Death Bird out and away from his beloved grandson.

Then he remembered that the Spanish doctor had definitely insisted that Jamie have a steady supply of fresh air. He had to leave the windows open.

So certain was Dennis that the White Bird of Death was coming that night, he was afraid to leave the windows to go for help. He couldn't yell for help, for fear of disturbing Jamie's troubled sleep. He had to fight the bird himself.

At daylight the next day, the doctor from Spain came into the room to find Jamie much improved and wanting breakfast. Dennis O'Neal was on the floor in front of the only open window, dead. Both hands were clenched around strange, long, and beautiful white feathers.

The learned doctor decided that Dennis had died of a heart attack. But the people of the village knew that he had given his life to keep the White Bird of Death away from Jamie. The bird wouldn't leave until it had a soul. Therefore it had taken his soul when he wouldn't let it get past him to Jamie.

The number of O'Neals alive today shows that Jamie did recover and was able to carry on the family name.

# 7. The Godmother

ONCE THERE was a man and a woman who had a young baby, whom they wanted to have baptized. Not knowing anyone well, they started to look for a godparent. After a while they met the devil, who offered to be the godfather, but the parents objected because he was evil and ugly.

Then they met an old woman with a sickle, who said she would like to be the child's godmother. The man and woman knew that the woman's name was Death, but since she took the lives not only of good people but also of bad, thought that she was all right. After she baptized the baby, the woman said that, although she had nothing to give the child, she would give the father something. She told him that she would give him the power to become a doctor. The man could not understand it, because he knew nothing about doctoring, but did as she said anyway. The old woman told him to go into town, and get himself an office, and tell everyone that he was a doctor, which he did. She also told him that when he went to see a sick person, he was not to worry, because if the person were going to die, he would be able to see her shadow behind the door.

So the man set up his business and did what the godmother said. Every time he saw the old woman's shadow behind the door, he would tell the family of the sick person that the patient was going to die, and he would.

The man did this for many years and became very rich. But one day he got sick and was in bed when he saw the old woman's shadow behind the door. He asked her what she was doing in his room, and she told him that it was time for him to die.

The man, being frightened, covered his eyes and would not look at the shadow, and because of this, kept from dying. This went on for a few days, until one day his daughter brought her new baby into his room for him to see. She told her father to look, for she had found someone to baptize her child.

When the father looked, there in front of him stood the old woman with the sickle.

## 8. The Devil, Death, and Simon Greene

ONCE UPON a time a village blacksmith named Simon Greene was sitting in his wine cellar drinking a glass of his favorite beverage when Death appeared in the doorway and told him it was time for him to go with her. Simon

Greene didn't want to die so soon and tried to think of a way out. Finally he asked Death if she would join him in his last glass of wine. She accepted not just one glass but several, and soon was bragging about how she could change herself into anything in the world. Simon Greene asked her if she could change herself into anything small enough to fit in his wine keg. She scoffed and said she certainly could; with that she decreased her size and crawled into the keg. Without a moment's hesitation Simon grabbed up the keg and placed a cork in it.

Death screamed and cried in agony for him to let her out, but he refused and placed the keg on the shelf. The years slowly passed and no one died. Crippled and sickly people roamed the streets of the town, praying that they could die, but nothing happened because Simon Green still had Death locked up in a keg in his cellar. This continued for seven years and Simon, who was tired of seeing these miserable people, decided to let Death go; but before he did, he made her promise that she would never come for him again. Death was so frightened and so glad to be free that she promised never to bother him again. Then she went back to heaven. Time and again after she had returned, God asked her to get Simon Greene, but she refused.

One alternative was left. God would send the devil after Simon. The devil went to earth and tried to enter the blacksmith shop and capture Simon Greene unawares, but a cross hung over the door of the shop and the devil could not enter. Near the back of the shop was an open window through which the devil could enter, but unknown to him was the fact that the blacksmith had seen him and was prepared for him. Just as the devil was ready to jump he saw Simon holding a burlap sack under the window, but it was too late—the devil was in the sack.

Simon Greene placed the sack on his anvil and began to pound as hard as he could with a steaming hot iron. The devil screamed and pleaded with Simon to let him out, but Simon kept on beating. Finally Simon grew tired and told the devil that he would let him go if he would never blacken his door again. The devil agreed and returned to Hades.

Years passed and Simon Greene grew older and older, only to face the future and know that nothing mattered to him anymore. His family and friends were dead and he was old and ready to die, but Death would not come for him. Simon could not bear to live any longer, so he decided to seek Death. He put all his belongings in a bag and started on his journey. When he reached the pearly gates of heaven he knocked and Saint Peter answered and asked him what he wanted. He told Saint Peter that he wanted to see Death, but when Death came to the door, she quickly ran away and said she never wanted to see him again. Saint Peter told Simon that he could not enter heaven, since he was not dead, so Simon decided to go see the devil.

When Simon Greene reached Hades, the devil came to the door to see if he had another helper, but when he saw Simon, he slammed the door and called all his trustees to help him hold it so that Simon could not enter.

Simon was completely lost. He could not enter heaven and the devil would not let him into Hades. Since there was nothing left for him on earth and he had to find a new home, he jumped across the sky and landed on the moon. Some say that on a clear night when the moon is full, you can see Simon Greene pounding on his anvil.

34

# *9.* Look in Your Own Backyard

THERE ONCE lived a happy, rich man whose name was John. He had everything life had to offer—many racehorses, a ranch full of cattle, a multitude of friends, a good wife to love him, and all the money he could ever spend.

One day Death came knocking on his door. When he answered the door, there she stood with her scythe on her back.

"Hello, old boy," she said. "Come along with me. It's time to go."

Being afraid of Death, he began to cry and beg for his life. "Please," he said, "I have a wife, friends, and money. Don't take me yet. Leave me here a few more years and I will give you all my money."

"No," said Death. "Where I come from, money is worthless; but if you have so many friends, go out and borrow some years from them. I will be waiting for you at midnight in the attic."

John thanked Death and started out to the houses of his friends. He went first to the home of his best friend, where he was greeted warmly. But when John explained why he had come, a frown crossed his friend's face.

"I'd gladly give you a couple of my years," he said, "but I am old and do not have much time left. Why not ask one of your younger friends?"

John thanked his old friend and left. He went to the home of one of his youngest friends and knocked on the door. His young friend greeted him warmly, but when he learned why John had come to see him, a frown crossed his face. He spoke softly.

"I'm sorry, John, I'd love to help you, but I'm young— just starting to live. I don't want to hasten my death."

John thanked him, assuring him that he understood, and left.

All day John walked the streets, going from house to house, calling on everyone he knew, but the answer was always the same. When night fell, he turned his broken spirits homeward. When he reached home, he was greeted by his wife. She was worried about him because he had been gone all day. John rushed to her arms, sobbing, and told her of his trying experience.

John's wife kissed him tenderly and said, "My poor darling, you didn't have to walk the streets all day for that. You know that I would gladly give you half of the rest of my life."

"Oh, no," he said. "I could never take your life, not even a small portion of it."

"But, John," she pleaded, "I couldn't bear to live without you."

Finally John was persuaded to take half of her life, and Death had to leave without her victim.

# Vampires and Werewolves

## 10. The Curse of the Vampire

PART ONE: Alexandru Capak and his young wife, Maria, left Bucharest in 1816 for their summer vacation. Their visit was to take them into the hills of Transylvania where the Capaks had many relatives. It was a short journey via the Romanian equivalent to the American buckboard on bumpy roads. In three days, they arrived at the country estate of Andre Capak who gave them a grand welcome. Tired from the long journey, they settled down for the night.

The next seven days were spent in festivity, laughing

and drinking, for the Capaks have always been champion bibbers. Their gaiety was short-lived, however, for Andre suddenly heard a blood-chilling cry from his wife, Theresa, in her bedroom upstairs. Andre rushed to his wife's side where he found her lying across the bed, lifeless.

A few hours later, when Andre finally came back to his senses, he began making funeral and burial arrangements. He arranged to have her remains buried in a certain plot on the estate where other members of the family had been placed in times past. Alexandru and Maria had planned to stay in Transylvania for the summer months, and, since Andre refused to leave his estate and go home with them, they remained there at his request.

Andre tried to discover what had killed Theresa, but the only clues were two tiny slits under her left cheekbone. That was all. When someone suggested that she had been the victim of a vampire, Andre went into a rage, for he knew such creatures couldn't exist. Besides, if this were true, he would have to dig up Theresa's body and drive a stake through her heart. No, Andre could not do this to his Theresa, and for a long time, her death was a mystery to both Alexandru and him.

Less than three months later, after Andre had recovered from the shock of the events, he was taking a solitary night walk on the grounds of his estate. A full moon was shining and he could see everything around him. As he walked further on, he thought he heard a soft voice calling his name. No, that was impossible. He was the only one out at that hour of the night. Then he heard it again.

"Andre, Andre, come to me Andre! Don't you know your own wife?"

Andre turned and, in the light of the moon, saw the

form of a woman. It sounded like Theresa, but it looked unbelievably pale and thin. As he approached the form to get a closer look, he realized the truth. It was Theresa.

"Andre," she said, "we are together again, but you must listen to me. You must get Alexandru and Maria off the estate immediately! If they know that I am seeing you, they might get suspicious."

And thus every night Andre and Theresa began seeing each other in secret. No matter how hard Andre tried, however, he could not get Alexandru and Maria to leave —without hurting their feelings. Therefore they remained.

During the next few months, Andre's health began to decline. He began to grow pale, his ruddy complexion fading away. There also seemed to be many deaths among the children and youth of Transylvania. When the dead were checked for "bad blood" by the local doctors, who were in truth barbers, it seemed as if something had drawn the blood from their veins beforehand. Moreover, there were usually two small slits under the cheekbones of these individuals. Some of the old wives began circulating a story about a vampire being on the loose, but the young intellects of the village scoffed át such talk.

Andre's health was still declining and Alexandru was quite worried. He was especially disturbed by his cousin's walk each night at eleven o'clock, but Andre became very angry if anyone asked to accompany him. For a long time, Alexandru had wondered if he were engaged in shady dealings. Finally, he followed him one night and discovered the truth. He recognized the pale and withered ghost of Theresa, who, as Andre was kissing her, was drawing the very blood from his veins. It was only then that Alexandru realized the cause of the deaths of so many people.

Fearing for his own life, he quietly hurried back to the house and began looking for a certain bush whose common name was "wolfsbane." (Wolfsbane is thought to be a perfect repellent to vampires, who become absolutely powerless in the presence of it.) He cut off a few stems and fastened them to the windows and doors of his and Maria's room. They were safe now. He cut off an extra piece of stem, took it to his room, and hid it in his belongings. Alexandru was now prepared for anything. As for Maria, she slept through all of it.

When Andre returned, he looked like an albino. He was so weak that Alexandru had to help him to his room.

"Let me get a doctor for you, Andre."

"No, no, I need no doctor," rebuked Andre, and he fainted on his own bed. Alexandru tucked him in and went to his room to prepare a few things. It was now clear that Theresa was a vampire, and, as a result of her bloodthirstiness, Andre was pining away; soon his fate would be identical to hers. Alexandru had to do something.

The next night, Andre's health seemed to have become amazingly better, and he left the house again. This time, Alexandru followed him, and in his coat was a piece of wolfsbane. When Andre met Theresa at the usual spot and began to embrace her, Alexandru leaped out of nowhere with the wolfsbane in his hand. But it was too late. Thresa had already put the finishing touch on Andre, thus making him a vampire like herself. At the sight of the leaves, they both seemed to disappear in a thick vapor. Hurrying back to the house, Alexandru realized that it was time for him and Marie to start back to Bucharest.

Somehow the word spread through the village about the incident, and the next day, before leaving, Alexandru went to the grave of Theresa. There he found Theresa's coffin, dug up and opened. Lying beside the coffin were two bodies, one almost decayed and the other still intact, both with stakes driven through their hearts.

PART TWO: When Alexandru Capak and his wife went to visit their cousins in Transylvania, they left their two-year old son, Peter, in Bucharest. When the cousins, Andre and Theresa, had fallen victims to the vampire curse, the visitors had left and had never gone back. All this had happened in 1816.

Twenty years later Peter had completed his schooling and was ready to leave Bucharest. He had always wanted to be an artist, and he did have talent in painting, especially in portraits and landscapes.

Peter was now twenty-two years of age and was allowed to lead his own life. In order to get a real masterpiece, he thought he should go to an unspoiled locality and paint things as they really were. What shocked his parents was that he wanted to go to Transylvania.

When they tried to tell him what had happened to his cousins, Andre and Theresa, he only laughed, saying that such things couldn't happen and that he was going to Transylvania, no matter what anyone said. After Peter had made arrangements to live on Andre's estate, he began packing his belongings. Since the Capaks were Catholics, they insisted that he take his rosary with him to shield him from evil.

A week later, Peter Capak made his exodus from Bucharest to Transylvania. The journey was slow, but in about three days he arrived at his destination. When the village people discovered who he was, they begged him to go back before he, too, met the fate of his cousins. But Peter was determined to "show these peasants" that he was not afraid of dead people. Realizing that Peter was headstrong, some of the villagers helped him move in.

Having settled down, Peter began to scout around the house. He went up to his room where his parents had been, when they had visited earlier. Into the room he walked and stopped. "What is that horrible odor?" he thought. Looking around him, he saw the source of the smell. Fastened to the window was a branch of the wolfsbane bush. Quickly he tore it off and discarded it. Then he decided to explore the rest of the estate.

As Peter was exploring the grounds, he came to the plot of ground where Andre and his wife were buried. He noticed that the coffins were not completely covered by the dirt. It was then that his curiosity got the best of him. He decided to dig up the coffins. What made Peter do such a thing, no one knows—even to this day—but he did. He went back to the house and in a short while came back with a shovel. It didn't take much digging to raise the coffins because the ground was soft and damp. When the coffins were raised, Peter opened them. There before his very eyes he saw two bodies with stakes driven through their hearts. It seemed that after the stakes had been driven through, they were cut off six inches above the skin in order that the bodies might fit into the coffins without propping the coffin lids up at any degree.

Suddenly Peter got the wild idea to pull the stakes from the bodies. As he pulled and tugged with all his might, it is said that the image of death smiled on him. When he finally dislodged the stake from Theresa's heart, he thought he heard a gasp of breath coming from her. But that was too fantastic. It was the wind. It had been cloudy and windy all day. Then he began to draw the stake from

42

Andre's heart. As the stake came out, he thought he heard another gasp of breath. Now, he realized that it *wasn't* the wind that he had heard. With a sudden turn on his heel, he dashed back to the house. Once he was inside, he prepared himself a drink to soothe his nerves.

The next day he hurried back to the burial grounds, but when he got there, the coffins were gone. All that was left were two short stakes and two empty graves. So, he assumed that he had been drunk the day before and that someone had stolen the two coffins and their bodies. His worries temporarily over, he put his shovel away, went back to the house, and set up his art equipment.

He began painting landscapes. As the weeks passed, he seemed to be building quite a reputation for himself as a painter. But all was not well within the village, for the death rate had begun once more, to climb. Autopsies determined the causes of the deaths to be heart seizures and extreme loss of blood. In most of the cases two small slits were found on the left cheekbone of each corpse. This caused the old wives' tales, as usual. Peter, of course, scoffed at them.

One night in early November, Peter was walking alone in the pale moonlight. Patches of white clouds were flowing across the moon. A slight but chilly breeze was blowing. In the distance could be heard the baying of a wolf. As fate would have it, Peter was strolling down the country road that passed by the village cemetery. As he walked by, he looked thoughtlessly at the tombs. Suddenly he saw something that startled him beyond measure—the form of a woman, sitting on one of the tombstones. Quietly he crept up to the fence to get a better look at her.

"Good evening, Peter," said a soft, feminine voice. "Come and talk to me."

Somehow Peter got over the fence and dashed to her side. "You *know* me? I don't know you!"

"Never fear. I am your friend."

"Here, take my coat. It's too cool out here with nothing on."

"No, I like it better this way. We must talk quickly. I haven't much time."

"But wait! Who are you and what do you want of me?"

"I *was* Ramona Metternich, and I'm attracted to you because you are so handsome and ruddy."

As she said those words, she began to disappear in a mist. Peter called out her name, begging her not to go, but as he called, he heard the baying of a wolf. Shaken up and tired, he hurried back to his room and went to bed.

The next day Peter thought continually of Ramona. She was so beautiful, he could think of nothing else. She looked to be in her early twenties—tall and blonde. Her skin was as pale as the moonlight itself. All day long he sat and dreamed. His inner voice compelled him to see her again. Therefore, the next night he left the estate and headed for the graveyard. With him he took his canvas and paints because he was determined to paint her portrait. For the first time in his life, Peter was in love. He did not know anything about this bewitching creature except that he loved her and felt he couldn't live without her.

When he arrived at the cemetery, Ramona was there, waiting for him. Placing his equipment on a tombstone, he sat and talked with her. As he talked, he said many soft, romantic words to her, since, like all the Capaks, he was quite good at expressing himself when it came to love-making. Finally he set up his art equipment and went to work. The painting was not completed in one night; it

44

took a fortnight. Each night as he would stop his work for the night, they would give each other a goodnight kiss. For some strange reason, Peter always felt limp and weak after that kiss, but he suspected nothing. At last, the painting was completed, and at first it looked perfect. But, as he looked at it more and more, there was something ghastly wrong with the image.

Meanwhile, back in Bucharest, Maria Capak was frantic. Her son had not kept in touch with her and Alexandru. She was almost sure that something had happened to him. Alexandru was worried, too, but he did not show it. He simply remarked that the vampires of Transylvania had been destroyed and there was nothing to worry about. But this did not stop Maria from worrying.

Then one day Maria became quite ill. When asked if she wanted anything special, she only replied that she wanted Peter and would rather die than have him gone. At once, Alexandru sent a message to Transylvania. A week passed, but Peter didn't show up. All this time, Maria was sinking fast. Alexandru sent another message, but to no avail. Before he could send a third message, Maria had aged a great deal and her hair had turned white from worry. Within a few days, she was dead. After her burial, Alexandru began planning a trip to Transylvania.

During the interim, some very strange happenings had taken place in Transylvania. Someone had sworn an oath that he had seen Peter with Andre and Theresa. The death rate of the children and young girls was climbing quickly in the surrounding territory. People had begun to wonder if Satan and his angels had been turned loose.

Alexandru wasted no time in making his trip to Transylvania. Upon his arrival, he inquired about Peter, and found out not only that he had taken ill and died but also that his body had disappeared. The villagers told him that Peter had been seen in the cemetery with a young woman every night before his death and disappearance.

Alexandru made haste to the Capak estate to begin his investigation of the unusual happenings. Once inside the house, he dashed into Peter's room. There he found the portrait that Peter had painted of Ramona. When he looked at it, he thought that he saw the teeth of a wolf in the mouth of the image. Quickly he ripped off the canvas and discarded it. Also, he realized that the wolfsbane branches had been cut from the window and door of that room. Tired from the long day, he decided to retire for the night and resume the investigation the next day. As he lay on the bed with its hard mattress, he sank into a dreamless slumber.

Late that night, he was awakened by a creak in the boards of the floor; it was after midnight. Lighting a candle, he looked up and saw what resembled his son. But the figure looked very thin and frail. At last, Alexandru spoke.

"Peter, my son, is it really you? It's been so long . . ."

"Yes, Father, it is I. You must come with me!"

"No, Peter, not yet. You must eat with me before we go. You look as if you have been starving . . ."

"No time for that! We must go now. A coach is waiting for us."

As Alexandru was dressing, he turned to the mirror. As he was checking his grooming, he noticed something. The mirror was large and it reflected practically the whole room and everything in it, but there was the reflection of only one person. According to the mirror, only one person was in that room—Alexandru. But when Alexandru turned around to look behind him, Peter was standing directly beside him, almost touching him; still there was only one image in the mirror. That proved it! Peter was definitely a vampire. Putting on his clothes, Alexandru bade Peter to wait outside for him in the coach.

Alexandru had a plan. It was too late to save Peter now, but he could save the people of Transylvania from this curse. Putting his cloak around him, he slipped outside and searched for the wolfsbane bush. Finding it, he cut off a few short stems and concealed them under his cloak. Then, he went to the coach where Peter and two other people were waiting. As Alexandru approached the coach, Peter spoke.

"Father, I would like for you to meet my wife, Ramona."

"Pleased to meet you, Ramona."

"The pleasure is all mine, sir."

Even as they spoke, Alexandru thought that she looked as bad as Peter did. He climbed into the coach with Peter and Ramona, and the driver began to race the vehicle toward its destination. Within two hours, the coach came into view of a castlelike structure, and there, it stopped.

"This is where all of us live," said Peter. "I would like for you to meet some of our friends who live with us."

As they walked through the entrance, one by one, Alexandru almost cringed at what he saw. There before his very eyes he saw the withered apparitions of his cousins, Andre and Theresa.

"What do you want of me?" cried Alexandru.

"We must have more blood," they said. "And you

will get it for us, or else you will become a vampire like the rest of us!"

Alexandru, jerking the wolfsbane from his cloak, firmly shouted, "That's what you think!"

At that, they all began to back off because wolfsbane rendered them powerless. Looking toward the window, Alexandru realized that it was dawn. If he could only hold them until the sun came up, he could destroy them and get rid of the danger.

Suddenly two of them made a dash for the door. The others followed. Alexandru ran outside after them. He saw a horse and jumped on it. Galloping after them, he chased them for a mile. Then they reversed on him and began to race back toward the house and safety before sunrise. (Vampires are destroyed if they are touched by a single ray of sunlight.) He chased them until they were about 500 feet from safety. All of a sudden, the sun began to rise. All of them stopped in their tracks and fainted. Alexandru jumped from the horse, ran to Peter, and carried him into the house and safety. But Peter was weak. Alexandru, with tears in his eyes, asked, "My son, why did you do this?"

In a weak voice, Peter told him everything that had happened—how he dug up the graves, how he met Ramona, and how she drew his blood from him, eventually making him a vampire.

Finally, he ended up by saying, "Please, Father take me outside. "It'll be better this way."

Alexandru, not knowing what he meant, followed his son's wish. The very moment the sunlight hit Peter directly, his flesh rotted from him, leaving nothing but a lifeless skeleton.

48

Sad, but relieved, Alexandru buried the remains of his son and also the rest of them, since their flesh had also rotted as the run rose. After burying the dead, he went back to Bucharest, hoping to forget this terrible experience which had plagued the Capaks—and the village in Transylvania—and had caused so many deaths.

# 11. Footprints in the Snow

In the quiet little village of Lutza in western Hungary lived Stefan Lutza, whose grandparents had founded the village over a hundred years before. Stefan followed the family tradition by becoming the mayor of the village that bore his name. It was the custom for the mayor to live in the big house that overlooked the village and to give shelter to all travelers that entered Lutza. But six years had passed, and no one had come to visit the mayor and his pretty young wife Esther.

Then one winter there came a knock on the door at midnight.

The snow was still falling as Esther got out of her warm bed. "I'll answer the door," she told her husband. "You go and see if the guest room is in order."

Stefan knew that he should be the one to answer the door and Esther to attend to the guest room, but he knew that she always was delighted when she met people for

49

the first time. So, without offering a word of protest, he wrapped a heavy robe around his body and headed for the guest room.

"I'll make him stay until the snow melts," Esther said to herself.

She didn't know why she knew the knocker was a man. She gave her hair an extra pat and then opened the door. Through the snow a tall, dark stranger emerged into the light of the room. The two figures stood silently for some time, and then, as if the whole thing had been agreed upon, Esther and the dark stranger departed into the falling snow.

Alarmed that she had not appeared with the guest, Stefan called out for his wife. Getting no reply, he dropped his robe on the floor and hurried down the single flight of stairs. The door was wide open and white snowflakes fell lazily on the floor. From the lamp he was holding he could see tiny footprints leading down the winding path. Stefan followed them, walking for nearly an hour before he realized that he, too, was barefooted.

He swung the lantern around and discovered he was in the village graveyard. Frightened, he ran more feverishly than ever along the single track of footprints, until they entered one of the tombs. Even before Stefan opened the wooden casket, he knew that the tomb belonged to his family. The casket lettering read, "Piztau Lutza, 1782-1852, settled and founded the village of Lutza in 1799." It was empty, except for shredded black rags that had once served as the clothing of his grandfather.

What happened that night Stefan could never say for sure. When he finally got back to the house, he was so tired that he decided to get some sleep and continue the search in the morning. As he lay on the bed, he was aware of somebody breathing beside him. Grabbing the lantern, he held it close to the breathing figure. It was his wife Esther!

"What is it, Stefan?" she said, sitting up. Then noticing his red feet, she said, "Where have you been?"

Had Stefan been only dreaming and imagined all this? But how did the tomb door get opened? And how did the single footprints get in the snow, and how did the tiny red marks get on Esther's neck?

The figure Esther described, the one she had seen in her dreams, was that of Piztau Lutza, a man who had been dead for over a hundred years.

# *12.* Old Man Devaule

MANY YEARS AGO, there was an old shepherd called Devaule, who lived alone in a little cottage on top of Mount Zenta. Whenever he was asked about his life, he always told the same gruesome story.

When he was twenty-one years of age, he married one of the prettiest maidens in the village. She gave birth to a beautiful baby boy, who grew straight and strong until he was fifteen. Then, one day while working in the field, he died without a cause. Devaule's wife could not bear the loss of her only son, and within two years, she had grieved herself to death. The shepherd was left to live alone.

Every night when lying awake in his bed, he would hear strange noises outside his window, and a soft muffled cry of, "Father, Father, come here!"

When he went to the window no one would be there, but he always saw drops of blood on the windowsill. This went on every night for nearly a month.

Finally, he decided to find out what was happening outside his window. One night, just after dark, he hid behind some bushes and watched. He looked toward the sky, where the moon was shining brightly, and saw a large bat—about the size of a man. The creature circled the house twice and landed near the window. Before the old man's eyes, it changed into a form that resembled his dead son. At first he thought the moonlight was playing tricks on his eyes.

His son—or whoever or whatever the form was—looked grotesque. He was dressed in black, with a pale, dead-looking skin, and blood dripping from his fingers. Devaule, shocked at seeing such frightening features, gave a small, terrified cry. The strange form whirled around to see who was behind him. Maddened at the thought of being spied upon, he charged at the older man.

Suddenly he stopped. He seemed to recognize the man. Before Devaule could recover from his fright, the figure turned back into a bat, leaped up into the sky, and flew off into the distance.

Devaule never again heard mutterings outside his window.

# 13. Ivan

IVAN WAS BORN and brought up in a small town in Hungary. He was a big, goodlooking boy, who could do everything well. He had a large farm on the outskirts of town and was engaged to the prettiest girl in the village.

Ivan was very happy. Then came the war, and he was drafted into the army. He went to war and was wounded in the head. When he returned to the village, he was no longer the same person.

He acted like a child. All the people in the village made fun of him and took advantage of his great strength by getting him to do their work for them. The girl's family would not allow her to see him in his present condition. Ivan began to spend more and more time away from the village. He began to roam the hills like an animal.

One day in his wanderings in the mountains he came upon a witch. Seeing that he had a way with animals, she began to tell him how wonderful it would be to be an animal. He agreed, so she called the devil, who made him sign a pact. In return for giving his soul to the devil, Ivan was to have the power to turn into a werewolf when the moon was full.

On the first night of the full moon, a reign of terror started in Ivan's village. Three people were found with their throats torn out and the blood drained from their bodies.

The older people of the village knew what this meant— that someone had made a pact with the devil. In the

following months more and more of the villagers were killed. The people of the village on different occasions saw the werewolf, a large beast, heading back to the hills where Ivan was now staying.

A council of the elders met and decided that someone must go into the hills on the next night of the full moon, with a gun loaded with silver bullets. The first night they sent out a man, but the following day he was found dead, with the gun unfired. This happened three times in a row. The werewolf was too sly to let the villagers see him before he killed them.

Ivan's girl, Tina, went before the council and asked that she be allowed to try. The council, now desperate, agreed. That night Tina, armed with a small pistol loaded with silver bullets, set out for the hills. She began climbing higher and higher into the mountains. Suddenly she heard a noise behind her, and turning, saw a large wolf. The wolf looked at her and a flicker of recognition came into his eyes. He walked up close to Tina; she pulled out the gun and shot him.

Upon being shot, a transformation came over the wolf. He turned back into the Ivan of old. He told Tina of his pact with the devil and asked her to help him. Tina took out her rosary and said a prayer over the dying man. Then he began saying it with her, driving the devil from his soul. Ivan was now free to die and go to heaven. Tina, seeing the love of her life dying, turned the gun on herself and pulled the trigger.

The next morning the villagers found them lying locked in an embrace, with a smile upon their faces. Now they would spend eternity together.

# 14. The Lady Was a Werewolf

SOMEWHERE IN the countryside of Romania, in a little village called Cluj, lived a family by the name of Mestrovic. They had no children, although they were in their late twenties and were quite well-to-do. Being young and likeable, they were usually surrounded by callers at all times of the day. Every once in a while, they would have a social gathering and invite friends from some distance away. Usually at these gatherings the guests would stay all night.

One night in early May 1853 the Mestrovics were having such a party, and everything was going well. The ladies were exchanging the gossip of the week, and the men were getting drunker by the minute. Lorraine Mestrovic supposedly had gone to her room and her husband, Erich, was entertaining the guests with hardly any effort at all. During a lull among the masculine members of the party, one of the intoxicated gentlemen decided to go outside for a breath of fresh air. No one said anything to him, because no one was in a condition to talk to anyone about anything.

Suddenly the lull of the party was broken by a blood-curdling cry, which momentarily sobered all the men. Greatly motivated by the disturbances outside, Erich calmly stepped out into the patio to see what was going on and almost tripped over something. He gazed at the ground beneath him and saw what nearly made him sick with fright. At his feet, lying in a pool of blood, was the body of his friend who had gone outside for air. But who could have done this terrible deed? And why did it happen here? These were questions that raced through Erich's mind as he finally gained his senses. Turning quickly, he called for help. Some of the less intoxicated men came out and helped Erich drag the body into the house. One of them went to summon the constable of the area.

When the constable arrived and examined the body, he noted that it looked as if an animal had attacked the victim. His flesh was torn to shreds and his arm was nearly chewed in two. Upon seeing this, the ladies nearly fainted. A few minutes later, they heard a sound of footsteps and saw Lorraine coming down the stairs, wearing an evening dress. When asked if she had heard anything while she was upstairs, she replied that she had been asleep because of a headache.

As the next few days came and went, tension mounted in Cluj, and the people began to panic. Tales were started. Some said that a bloodthirsty animal was loose; others said that it was a werewolf. In the village at the time was an old woman who lived alone and, according to gossip, sometimes did strange things. Without thinking, some of the younger group began circulating stories that the woman was a witch who could turn into a werewolf whenever necessary.

One night, Lorraine went outside to get some fresh air, since the house was poorly ventilated. She was gone some fifteen minutes. While she was outside, Erich was in the living room, drinking a glass of wine. Suddenly he heard a scream from outside. Realizing it was the voice of Lorraine, he sped to her assistance. There in the patio he found his wife, nearly in hysterics, standing over a bloody mess.

It was the same result as that of the party. Once again he called for the constable and had the body removed. When he asked Lorraine what had happened, she replied that an animallike figure in the clothes of an old woman had committed the act. This caused much disturbance because attention was beginning to center around the old woman who was believed to be a witch. Some advocated burning her at the stake while others who were more peaceful advised running her out of the village.

Each night, there was a new victim. Quite often the slaying happened on the patio of the Mestrovics. At that point, people were getting furious. Could nothing be done to curb these disasters? This seemed to be the question of the hour. The whole village was in an uproar. The constable seemed to be useless in this case; he could do nothing to curb the killings that were taking the population by storm. Also, the people were beginning to riot and to endanger the life of the old woman. To make matters worse, the stories about her queer ways were being exaggerated and few people actually knew the truth from the exaggerations.

One night, as things were mounting up to a horrible climax so far as the old lady was concerned, a strange thing happened. As Erich was drinking his nightly wine, he decided that *he* needed some fresh air. As he stepped out into the patio, he was horror-stricken with what he saw. There, before his very eyes, he saw the form of a wolf in a young woman's clothes, attacking one of the villagers.

Frightened almost to death, he ran back inside and seized his old gun. Outside, the wolflike figure was still at work. Standing in the doorway, Erich took aim with the gun and fired at the creature. When the smoke cleared away, he saw, beside the mutilated body of the villager, the body of his wife, with a bullet through her head.

# *15.* The Werewolf of Campobello

TO PLANTERS and astronomers, a full moon may mean good sky-watching and planting, but to the citizens of Campobello, it meant nights of terror. Among the people in the village was a man named Angelo Schemari, who was the caretaker at the local schoolhouse in the village. He was especially good at caring for roses and had them growing all over the school grounds. Some of these flowers were prize possessions. There were some species that no one had ever seen before. He possessed a real green thumb as far as roses were concerned.

Angelo, however, was the victim of a strange behavior. Usually he seemed perfectly normal, but every month on the night of the full moon he changed completely. Everyone in Campobello watched the coming of the full moon with terror. They knew these nights belonged to Angelo and his strange state of mind. Everyone was on the lookout for him at such times, for on that particular night he would quietly leave his family without telling them where he was going and walk to the crossroads on the outskirts of town. He would crouch down in the shape of a wolf, look up at the moon, and begin howling.

It was a weird and mournful cry. My grandmother said that it was of such strength, that on a quiet evening, its echo could be heard in the next village. He also made terrible noises, and his face took on the look of an animal, with terrible contortions. He would be there for hours, howling at the moon, waiting for a human to pass by.

After several hours of howling, if no one came by, he would go from house to house in the village, looking for one with a light in it. The light reminded him of the moon. He would scratch on the door, a weird, clawing scratch, and then begin howling. He wanted someone to come out, just anyone, as long as it was another human.

There was a reason behind his strange actions. He could only be relieved of this unusual behavior by bleeding profusely. The bleeding would have to be caused by a human, either by cutting or scratching. He wanted someone to fight with him so he could receive the bleeding during the fighting engagement. Only in that way could he lose his wolf-tendencies and return home to his family.

It was a very brave person who would let himself become involved in a struggle with Angelo. Some who were really brave and strong went out in two's and four's and gave him a good whipping and a few good gashes so they could be rid of him and let him go home. After he began bleeding, he would become calm and head for home, where his wife would be waiting to dress his wounds and put him to bed. Then everything was calm until the next night of the full moon.

Since most of the folks in the village knew how he was to be relieved of this spell, most people were in their homes with the doors locked and the shades pulled down tight. His attacks were wolflike and he didn't care whom he attacked. It could have been a woman, a child, or someone who was old and senile. If they did not scratch him and make him bleed, he would fight on. Some of the people he attacked were beaten badly.

No one killed him because they felt sorry for him, and his family was liked and respected in the community. Since they believed in witchcraft, they thought killing him would pass the curse on to them. Usually his victims were strangers in the town who knew nothing about him. Often he would howl at these same crossroads for hours until a stranger finally came upon him quite unknowingly and was attacked. Most strangers thought he was a drunk who was in a state of stupor or shock.

My great-grandmother said that she can remember quite well as a child how the nights of the full moon were filled with terror. Everyone had to be home to await the howls and scratches of the "Werewolf of Campobello." It was a sad situation, especially for his family, who were fine people. I asked her if she knew how Angelo was endowed with this unusual power, and she said that he was probably bewitched by someone who was capable of putting such curses on people. In that town, a lot of the townsfolk believed in witches and spells.

# *16.* The White Wolf

IN A LITTLE Hungarian village, strange happenings occurred that had the people living in a state of fear. Every night for several weeks a murder had been committed. The victims were of all ages and of both sexes. The only clues found were the mutilated bodies of the victims.

The first victim was a young girl about eighteen years old. The authorities found her lying in a small area, which at present we would consider a park. Her hair was tangled and caked with blood. Her throat and face had long scratches, which looked like claw marks.

The next victim was an old man, and when he was found, his body was in the same position and condition as that of the young girl. The little village was in an uproar, and its occupants ran for shelter at dusk. The people were frightened because of these unusual murders, and they had every right to be.

As the murders became more frequent, witnesses had related that they either saw a white object running away from its victim or heard a loud, shrill cry. Now the people knew that someone or something stalked at night, killing for no apparent reason.

The men of the village gathered guns and weapons, which could be used to fight the beast. They set up a system so that all the men would take turns, watching for the appearance of the "white phantom."

In one particular household, these murders became the main topic of discussion. The occupants of this house were an elderly man, his three sons, and a lovely young daughter. The man treated his children as if they were infants; and, after his wife's death, which hadn't been over a year before these murders took place, he became harsh and cruel. His children didn't understand his reasons for doing the things he did, but they knew it concerned the mysterious death of their mother. Lately he had been acting strangely, taking long walks at night and sitting silently by the fire during the day.

One evening after the man went for his usual walk, his eldest son followed him. He walked cautiously, making sure his father didn't hear him, and from behind the large oak tree in the center of a clearing, he saw his father take the huge form of white wolf. The wolf sat on its haunches, waiting for its prey to pass by. After a short time, the image of the boy's dead mother appeared before the wolf and started talking. The boy saw a haze gather around both objects and a strange whistling noise seemed to fill the air.

Suddenly the image disappeared as swiftly as it had appeared. The boy turned quickly toward the direction of the village. Instantly he knew why the image had disappeared. His mother was conspiring with his father against the villagers. Her revenge was evidently connected with her death.

At the moment the image disappeared, a little boy about twelve years old bounced his rubber ball into the clearing. The youth saw his father attack the child and tear him to shreds. The son drew his rifle to his shoulder, aimed, and shot the white wolf, as it was changing into the form of a man.

No longer would his village be plagued with the mysterious murders performed by the white wolf.

# *17.* Ears Can Give You Away

ONE NIGHT a man named Martin was waiting in an English train station. The night was unusually dark, and the train was late. Mr. Martin was getting extremely worried and was starting to shake with fear.

He finally decided that he had to talk to someone, and he saw at his far right a tall man in a trenchcoat and a hat over his eyes, who was staring at the floor. When he approached the man and said that he had to talk to someone, the man told him to start talking.

Mr. Martin told his story, saying it had all started when he got a message from his father telling him to come home, which was in the country, because all his sheep were being killed. When he got home his father showed him the tracks they had traced from previous raids. First they were wolf tracks, but farther on in the field the tracks were human. This was the reason he had sent for his son.

Then his father had told him that there was something very important that he should know. He explained that he had an older brother whom he had never seen. He went on to say that when his brother was born, he was rather deformed-looking. He had pointed ears, slanting green eyes, and forefingers longer than his middle fingers. They were planning to destroy him, but one of the maids took the baby, and the parents never saw him again.

The father advised Mr. Martin to leave and never return, since he felt sure his brother was a werewolf, who would resent the idea of receiving no inheritance, and would probably stop at nothing to get revenge.

Turning to the man in the station, Mr. Martin said, "And this is why I am here. I do wish the train would hurry, so I can go far, far away." Then he asked the stranger if he believed such a ridiculous story, and the man said, "Yes."

Amazed, Mr. Martin exclaimed, "But why should you believe it?"

The man looked up, took his hands out of his pockets, and removed his hat. His ears were pointed, his green eyes were slanted, and his forefingers were longer than his middle fingers.

# 18. The Secret

THE SMALL TOWN was awaking to a bright, sunlit day. The older citizens were seated in front of the town's only inn, enjoying the warmth of the early spring sun. The peaceful scene was disturbed by the loud barking of dogs. They followed at the heels of a stranger, who called to a group of playing children and inquired about lodgings.

Given directions, he turned toward the inn. He could see the older men study him as he approached them. Not many tourists stopped in the small town, and they wondered what was bringing him here.

The stranger was in his late thirties. He had thick brown hair that grew low over his forehead. His skin looked leathery and weatherbeaten. A pack, containing all his possessions, was slung over his shoulder. The dust of the road made his clothing look gray.

Isabelle, the innkeeper, was surprised when the man walked in and asked for lodgings. She gave him the best room to please him and hoped his stay would be long. The girl was lonely since her father's death, and she longed for company. Somehow she felt drawn toward the stranger, a feeling she could not explain.

No one seemed to know anything about the new lodger and were amazed and concerned when Isabelle announced one night that she and the man were going to be married.

The wedding was a quiet affair, and after the last guest had left, Nicholas told his new bride he had something to tell her. "On my twenty-first birthday, a spell was cast upon me by my old spinster aunt. Every month when the moon is full, a restlessness comes upon me, and I must spend the nights roaming the countryside. You must not be afraid, for no harm will come to you if you will do as I say. Never unlatch the door if you hear scratching upon it. If I knock three times, that means the spell is broken and you need not fear."

One bright, moonlit night, Isabelle was awakened from her bed, where she was sleeping peacefully, by the loud barking of dogs and voices outside her window. She ran downstairs to see what was causing all the commotion. She could hear loud scratching on her door, and she remembered her husband's warning.

She waited, not knowing what to do, when a shot was heard, and the scratching stopped. She threw the door open, and there at her feet lay a figure that looked half-man and half-beast. Slowly before her horrified eyes, the image of the wolf was gone, and in its place was her dying husband. She cradled his head in her arms and heard his last words, "Don't tell the secret."

Time has gone by and no one knows the whereabouts of Isabelle. The boarded-up inn is slowly crumbling and all that remains of this tale are the ugly, deep scratches on the heavy wooden door.

# *19.* Fatal Shortcut

MY FATHER'S FAMILY certainly had their share of misfortunes; first it was his young sister Esther who came to a mysterious death, and then it was his older brother, Steve. It seems strange, having two such deaths in a single family, but in Old Hungary anything could happen, and it usually did.

Steve was in his third year of high school when tragedy struck the Puskas family for the second time within a year. The children were all playing games behind the barn when Steve's mother called to him. She wanted him to take the butter and milk to the village and exchange them for money. My father wanted to go with his older brother, but Steve refused. "Go back and play with the rest of the children," he said.

Steve kissed his mother on the cheek, picked up the butter and milk, and took off toward the village. What happened after that nobody will ever know. Steve always took the same shortcut through the woods, but this was to be his last trip. Hearing screams, my grandfather and father ran quickly in the direction of the loud noise. Steve was lying in a clump of bushes, and his appearance was almost unrecognizable. At first, my grandfather thought he had been attacked by some wild animal, but the only tracks were those of a man.

It was dark before my grandfather and father reached home. Just before they reached the clearing, they heard a howling sound. A cloud was covering the moon, but when the cloud passed, they discovered, in the light of a full moon, that the howling creature was no more than twenty feet away from them. My father didn't see it clearly, but my grandfather swears that it was a werewolf. He said it was the same creature that had killed his son Steve. My grandfather and father will never be able to say for sure just what the creature really was, because they didn't stay around to find out.

The next day the villagers got together to try and track down the creature that my grandfather had described to them. When night came, they were about to give up the hunt. All they had found that day were a couple of wild bears and several deer, but no werewolf—not even tracks where my grandfather and father had seen the creature the night before. As they came to the clearing, the same howling sound appeared. One man said he saw the werewolf, but he mentioned that some weeks later. When the men heard the howling sound, they scattered in all directions. So nobody actually saw what the creature really was.

Until his death, however, my grandfather swore that when the moon was full he saw the half-man, half-wolf—not more than ten yards away.

# IV

# Evil Spirits, Curses, and Witchcraft

## 20. Seven Bones

A LONG TIME ago in Czechoslovakia, a young girl, whose mother was dead and whose lover had gone to war, went to an elderly fortuneteller to find out whether her lover was dead or alive. The old lady told her to get seven bones from seven different graves and boil them in a pot of water until midnight for seven nights. She said that at midnight on the seventh night her lover would come to her. If he were alive, he would be on foot, but if he were dead, he would be riding a horse. If he were a good spirit,

the horse would be black, but if he were an evil spirit, the horse would be white.

About this time there was an epidemic in the country. So many people had to be buried that all old, unidentified graves were opened and the bones thrown out to make room for the newly dead. The girl did as she was told. She took seven bones from seven different graves and put them in a pot to boil each night. As the bones boiled, they said, "Putce, putce, putce," meaning, "Come, come, come."

On the seventh night the bones boiled harder and harder, and as the time neared midnight, they said louder and louder, "Putce, putce, putce," and suddenly the girl heard someone coming. She knew that it was her lover and that he was riding a horse. As she looked in the direction from which he was coming, she saw that the horse was white.

The old woman had told her to prepare seven bundles of cloth to take along and to take her rosary with her if she left home—so she did. When her lover asked her to get on the horse behind him, so they could ride away to be married, she did as she was told. As they galloped along, he said,

> "How the moon brightly shines,
> How the horse swiftly runs!"

And as they went farther and farther from home, he repeated the words, somewhat changed,

> "How the moon brightly shines,
> How the ghosts swiftly glide!"

Finally they came to a church and a cemetery, and the girl realized this was probably her lover's burial place.

When he asked her to get down, she suggested that he get down first so that he could help her, which he did. But she threw the seven bundles in different directions, and the spirit-lover tore each of them apart before he tried to pursue her. The girl got down on the opposite side of the horse, ran to a nearby cottage as fast as she could, went in, bolted the door, and hung her rosary over the doorknob.

In one corner of the cottage were some chickens, and on a bench, stretched out, was a dead man. The lover had reached the door by this time, and when he found it was bolted, he asked the dead man to unbolt it for him. The dead man replied that he, too, was an evil spirit and could not open the door because a rosary hung over the knob. The ghost-lover then went to one side of the cabin and started to try to scratch out the sides with his clawlike hands.

The girl turned to the chickens and begged the rooster to crow, so that the spirits would have to vanish, but the rooster said, "No, I won't crow for you. When you fed the chickens, you always chased the rooster away, so why should I help *you*?"

In the meantime the ghost-lover had called upon the dead man to help him claw out the side of the cabin, and he did. Again, the girl turned to the chickens and begged the rooster to crow, promising him, if he would, she would never again chase the rooster away when she fed the chickens.

So the rooster crowed, the ghost-lover vanished outside, the dead man lay back on his bench, and the girl was saved.

# *21.* Seven Devils

IN A SMALL village of peasant farmers and humble dwellings within Budapest lived a miller and his seven lovely daughters. Because he ground all the grain for the village, he was considered one of the wealthiest men in the community. Each of his seven daughters was beautiful, and the miller worked hard to provide the best for them.

He wanted husbands for them who would be rich and handsome. The oldest daughter was planning to be married to a gentlemen much older than she, but he was very wealthy. The miller approved of her choice and was proud that his daughter had made such a wise decision.

One day a caravan of gypsies came to the village in their heavily laden wagons which jingled as they moved slowly down the cobbled streets. Their olive complexions, jetblack hair, dangling earrings, and brightly colored costumes caused the villagers to stare with awe as several half-naked gypsy children ran laughing and screaming behind the wagon. Usually gypsies arrive in a village and leave within a few days, but they liked this village so much they decided to stay for a while.

One particular gypsy was a small, thin musician. He appeared strikingly handsome with one golden earring and a wide brimmed hat decorated with silver spangles. The musician presented a fine appearance as he played his guitar, and his dark eyes sparkled in their slanted structure. He had heard about the wedding of the miller's oldest daughter, whom he had been observing for some time.

He didn't love her, but he was attracted to her by her beauty and desired to play for her wedding.

He asked the miller if he could contribute his talents by playing his prized guitar at the wedding festivities. At first the miller agreed and was much impressed by the gypsy's appearance. He thought that the music would add gaiety to the celebration. But after much thought on the agreement, the miller feared that his neighbors might not approve of having a gypsy at the wedding. He decided he would have to tell the musician that while he appreciated his offer, plans had been made previously, without his knowledge, to hire another musician.

Meeting the gypsy on the street one day, the miller told him that he couldn't play for the wedding. The gypsy appeared hurt and persisted in urging his cause, hoping the miller would change his mind. Realizing the man would not consent to his playing, the gypsy decided he would have to use witchcraft. He told the miller that if he couldn't play for the wedding, he would place a horrible curse on each of the daughters. In seven years the miller would lose them all, because they would be led by seven devils. The plans for these misfortunes were not revealed, but the gypsy inferred that each loss would be a tragedy. The miller felt as if the whole thing were some joke, and laughed in the gypsy's face. He turned and left, leaving the gypsy standing on the cobbled street with his guitar in his hands and an ugly sneer on his face.

Soon the gypsy caravan left the village, and the eldest daughter married as planned. After a year of happiness a baby was born, but the miller's daughter died in childbirth. The first phase of the curse had been carried out. Her rich husband then married the miller's second daughter and gave the child to his parents to care for. Soon after

74

their marriage the second daughter became a woman of ill-repute and ran away from the village.

The next three daughters died a year apart by incidents, not of natural causes. The miller became so frightened that he tried to shelter his two younger daughters, and he forbade them to marry. All his efforts were in vain, for they married gypsies and they, like the musician, left the village to roam the countryside. The musician never returned to the village and was never heard of again.

The curse had been fulfilled at the end of seven years as the gypsy had predicted, all because a miller denied a small, frail gypsy the glory of playing his guitar.

This tale is known throughout Budapest and all Hungary and serves as a warning to persons mistreating gypsies.

## 22. Javo's Curse

IN THE LANGUAGE of the Yugoslavians the word "Javo" means a promoter of death, or someone associated with ill omens of death, or death itself. The word also corresponds to all the misfortunes that might happen to an individual.

One day while walking through the country, a young man by the name of Duchien met Javo. Duchien was thoroughly amused by his extraordinary slim build, his uncanny slanting black eyes, and his starved appearance. He looked at Javo and could not restrain his laughter.

Javo became very angry and, with a glance into the eyes of Duchien, put a curse on him.

He looked at Duchien and said, "You shall never be happy again, and furthermore, if you should ever marry, you shall die."

A feeling of numbness went through Duchien, because he knew by the expression on Javo's face that he meant what he said. Duchien walked away, a very confused and frightened man.

He returned to his home and family, and became an entirely different person. His face acquired a certain pallor and his eyes a definite hollowness. His weight went down considerably, and he walked around like one without life. Night after night he lay awake, because when he closed his eyes, the appearance of Javo was always present. Duchien's mother and father noticed the difference in their son and realized he was facing some serious illness— in mind or body.

After much discussion, the parents decided it would be wise to ask him frankly about his problem. Duchien was afraid to tell at first, but finally, after their urging, he told them about his encounter with Javo and the curse that had been inflicted upon him. His mother and father laughed heartily at such a fear, and took the fear so lightly that Duchien himself realized that it was foolish. They told him to get married if he wanted to; if Javo wanted someone to die, they would die for him.

Duchien became his old self. He took up the friendships he once had had, among which was a very pretty, modest young woman of whom he was very fond. He began escorting her to various social gatherings, and when they realized their love for each other, he asked her to marry him.

The date for the wedding was set and in all the preparation, no thought or mention was given to Javo. On the day before the wedding, Duchien wished to be alone and decided to walk through the neighboring woods. After walking a short distance he sat on a fallen tree. As he sat there drowsily thinking of his beautiful bride-to-be, a figure shyly and quietly stood before him. Breathlessly he looked up into the slanting eyes of Javo.

Javo repeated the curse and told Duchien he was anxiously awaiting his next victim. Duchien told Javo he wasn't worried, because he didn't believe him, and his mother and father believed even less, because they themselves said thy would die for him. Javo said that was all right with him, because he would still be able to get revenge on Duchien.

The next day the wedding took place. At the reception that night, Javo made his appearance. He went to Duchien's mother and father and said, "Well, are you ready to die?"

They looked at him in astonishment and said they didn't want to die; that they hadn't thought Duchien was telling the truth when they'd made the statement.

Javo then went to Duchien and told him he was going to die. Duchien told Javo again that his mother and father were going to die for him. Javo told him what his mother and father had said, whereupon Duchien became frightened and his mind became filled with horrible thoughts. He was going to die if no one else did.

Duchien walked outside and killed his mother and father.

$$\bar{v}$$

# Dragons, Giants, and Other Monsters

*23.* The Story of Hedgy

DURING THE TIME when the states were not united and people had to get special permission to go from one state to another, there lived two kings—King George of Pennsylvania and King Jimmy of West Virginia. King Jimmy's wife had a three-month-old baby and wanted to visit a friend in Pennsylvania, but we must remember that people were not allowed to cross the boundary line from one state to another. Nevertheless, King Jimmy took his family and started to make the journey with his horse and buggy.

When they reached the boundary of Pennsylvania, there stood a guard who did not want to let them cross the line. He said that if they should even try, he would kill them. He seized the woman and told the king to go back to his home. King Jimmy would not agree to this, and the two men started to fight. While the men fought, the wife prayed to God that her husband would win. However, blood was pouring from King Jimmy's head, and soon he was dead. During the fighting, the wife had hidden her little son beneath the hedges that were near. She was afraid the guard would kill the baby, just as he was trying to kill her husband.

After he had killed King Jimmy, the guard told the lady she must either marry him or be put to death. She said she would not be his wife and would rather die at once. He did not want to kill her, however, so he put her in the buggy, took her to her own home, and locked her in the basement. Then he set himself up as king in place of King Jimmy, telling the woman that, when she made up her mind to marry him, he would let her out. In the meantime, she was to have a slice of bread and a glass of water a day.

While the mother was in the basement, the little baby lay beneath the hedges. A mother deer heard the child crying and went over to see it. Not knowing what else to do, she lay down beside it so it could nurse. When the baby got enough milk, it stopped crying. The doe went away, but before dark she came back again to feed the baby. After each feeding, she would go back to her regular sleeping place in the woods.

A missionary who was staying in the woods at that time depended on the doe for his milk supply. All day he waited for her, but when she returned, she had no milk for him. He tried hard to get even a small amount, but there was none. He prayed all night long, because he had nothing else to live on but some greens which he picked in the woods.

After this had gone on for several days, the missionary decided to follow the deer and find out what was happening. Soon she started to run very fast, but the man was right behind. She stopped to look at him, but when he started to grab her, she turned and ran on much faster. However, he did not give up, but continued to follow. When the doe got near the hedges, she heard the baby crying and ran still faster. The missionary suspected something by this time and followed her to the place where the baby lay. Now he understood why she had not given any milk.

Although he had been fed, the baby still cried, so the man took him in his arms and carried him to his hut in the woods. He found a medal on the child with the initials of G. M., but he decided to call the baby Hedgy, since he had found him beneath the hedges.

In the meantime, Hedgy's mother was still a prisoner. She cried day in and day out, for she felt that her son would soon be dead—that the wild animals probably would eat him.

Since the missionary lived alone, he enjoyed Hedgy's companionship. Living in the woods as he did, he could not buy shoes or clothing for the baby, so he made clothes out of animal skins. The days went by and Hedgy and the missionary were very happy together. During the daytime, the man taught the little boy many things. When Hedgy was ten years old, he could read and write better than his teacher, and had read the few books the man owned, many times. Since there was no paper to write on at that time or any pencils to use, they wrote with burnt sticks on flat pieces of rock.

The missionary told Hedgy all he knew about him. He told him how he found him, and took him to the spot. He told him he was not his father, but loved him as much as if he were. He gave Hedgy the medal that he had found on him when he was a baby.

When Hedgy was about fifteen years old, the missionary said one day, "I will not live much longer. My time is getting short."

Since Hedgy had not seen or even heard of death, these words made little impression upon him.

One morning the missionary did not get up. He just lay still in the place where he slept. Hedgy, not realizing what had happened, arose and fixed the morning breakfast for both of them. When everything was ready, he went to the bedside and shook the missionary but there was no response.

The day passed and night came. Hedgy went to bed again, and, when he arose in the morning, saw that the missionary was still asleep. He tried his best to awaken him, but again there was no response. He tried moving him about, but the missionary was stiff and cold.

Hedgy did not know what to do, so he started to cry. Then he remembered what the missionary had told him about dying. He thought about it all day long. Night came, and he went to bed. In the morning he got up and still did not know what to do. Finally he dug a hole and buried the missionary. Since the deer had died some time before, Hedgy was left all alone. He cried day and night for a long time.

Then one morning he heard someone calling, "Hedgy—Hedgy—Hedgy"; he looked around to see where the sound came from. He looked up in a tree, but at first saw nothing. He kept looking until he saw a little bird in another tree, and it started to sing again, "Hedgy—Hedgy—Hedgy."

Hedgy followed the bird and came to a road, about five hundred yards from where he lived. He walked on and on, following the bird that kept calling, "Hedgy—Hedgy—Hedgy."

Finally he came to a place where he heard a continual noise. He saw horses outside, but could not understand what they were. He had never seen a horse in his life before. He was still wondering what the noise was, and wanted to see what was on the inside of the place. He went to the door and looked in. There he saw men working, but did not know what they were doing. They were dressed in shoes and fine clothes, which seemed strange to him.

All the men stopped their work and looked at Hedgy. They noticed his bare feet, long hair, and queer clothing made from animal skins. Since they did not know what or who he was, they asked many questions of all kinds. He seemed to be well educated.

The men called him inside and talked further with him. The building was a factory where spears were made. The manager asked him if he were hungry and gave him a sandwich. Although Hedgy did not know what it was, he took it and ate it, explaining that it was the first time he had eaten anything like that. They asked him what he had eaten before, and he told them of his usual milk and greens. They gave him more sandwiches and he ate them.

They invited him to stay for dinner and asked him if he would like a haircut. He told them he would like all this very much. Some of them asked him where he came from and who his mother and father were. He said that he had no mother and had never seen his father. The manager offered him a job, and he accepted it.

There was a boy in the factory by the name of Tom. Everybody made fun of him and kept him crying much of the time. Hedgy did not like to see anyone treated in this way. Besides, sometimes they made fun of him too. Consequently, he decided to stop such actions. He fought with one of the men and, after a few blows, knocked him down. A second man took sides with the first, and Hedgy treated him in the same way. The rest of them did not bother him any more, nor did they make fun of Tom. Tom and Hedgy became the best of friends.

The actual spear-making was done by experts. After six months had gone by, Hedgy asked the manager if he could make a spear. The manager said, "How could you do such a thing, when you have had no instructions and know nothing about it?" He told him he would have to hit very hard.

While the blacksmith was giving him instruction, Hedgy hit with the hammer and broke it in two. The men gave him the steel and another hammer, and told him not to hit so hard. It was not long before Hedgy had a spear for himself. After he had made the first, he made another —even better than the. first. In making the second one, he had to use material that was very hard to work with. To the surprise of all the men, he had no trouble whatever in cutting it. His friend, Tom, was especially pleased.

With the spear, Hedgy cut down a tree that no one else could cut, and went back to the factory, taking with him the instrument, which, having been made from the best of material, was still in excellent condition. After this, even the manager was afraid of this strong man, and nobody dared to go against anything he said. They were all so surprised at his strength and fearful of what he might do to them that they wanted to get rid of him.

At that time people did not use coal. They used charcoal instead. They usually gathered this charcoal from a high hill that stood in front of the factory. However, it got so that nobody who went to the top of the hill ever came back down. The men thought if they could send Hedgy on the hill, he would never get back, and their worries would be over. They asked him to go, and he agreed.

Tom found this out and begged him not to go, but Hedgy said he would take his spear and kill anything he saw. Tom was afraid he would lose his best friend, but since Hedgy had made up his mind to go, nothing could stop him.

When Hedgy got to the top of the hill he heard a strange sound. At first he thought it was the wind. Then something jumped at him. Its head was as big as a bull. He hit it with the spear, but could not kill it. It jumped away for a while, and then came back. He hit it again and again, but his blows did not seem to go through its hide. He looked at the creature, but didn't know what to do. Then came the call, "Hedgy—Hedgy—Hedgy." He looked around to see what it was. There was the bird, who told him to hit the beast in the throat. The animal looked at Hedgy and Hedgy looked at it. Then he struck it in the throat and killed it.

He then heard the bird say, "Wash yourself with the blood, and nothing will ever hurt you."

After washing himself in the beast's blood, he took his spear and tried to cut himself, but could not. In one place a blackberry leaf had stuck to him, and when he pulled it off, he saw that his skin was white. He had

washed his entire body with blood—but had missed this small section! He pinched himself on the white spot and noticed that it hurt him. He looked for more blood, but could not find any.

The people at the bottom of the hill were all wondering what had happened. They thought by this time Hedgy was surely dead. Then they saw smoke on the hilltop and knew he was still alive.

When Hedgy came down from the hill, he brought the animal's head with him. He placed it on the floor and thanked the manager for sending him on the hill. The man asked him why he should thank him. Hedgy told about washing himself in the beast's blood—that he could never be hurt by anyone now. When Tom heard of this, he was very happy. He knew that since he was Hedgy's best friend nobody would ever try to hurt him again.

Hedgy's mother was still in the basement. A few years after the guard had imprisoned her, he had gone to her and asked if she was ready to marry him, but she would not even hear of it. Every time she saw him, it only reminded her of her husband and little son, whom she had left under the hedges. She asked the guard to kill her, just as he had killed her husband. He refused to do this, but decided to get himself another girl, marry, and start a family. He left orders that as long as the prisoner lived, she should have nothing but a slice of bread and some water each day.

By this time he was married and had children. He was still acting as king in place of King Jimmy and bringing up his family as if they were of royal blood. He let the prisoners of the city out of jail in order to help guard the palace and protect him. They liked this very much— especially being let out of prison. They liked him better than King Jimmy. As a result, the guard led the life of a king for quite a while, living happily, and having plenty of everything.

One day Tom invited Hedgy to meet his family—his parents, his sister, and a brother. When he was introduced, Hedgy looked at all of them strangely, because he had never seen a girl or woman in his life. Tom asked him why he looked so puzzled, but Hedgy did not tell him; he only said he didn't know. Tom's home was not in good condition. The furniture was somewhat worn and out-of-date, but Hedgy thought it was beautiful. He stayed with them for the night and thought everything was unusually fine. The bed was the best he had ever slept in. Tom and Hedgy slept together, but for some reason, Hedgy could not fall asleep. Tom asked him if anything was wrong.

Hedgy said, "Yes, but I'm ashamed to tell you. But, if you really want to know, I will."

He asked Tom why his mother, brother, and sister all dressed differently. Tom asked him what he meant. Hedgy pointed out that his brother and father had pants on like the two of them, but that his sister and mother didn't.

Tom said, "Don't you know why? They are women and my brother and father are just like you and me."

Hedgy didn't ask any more questions. He just thought and thought.

Soon morning came and they had breakfast. This was the best that Hedgy had ever eaten. A little later they had dinner and then started back to the factory to work. As they were walking to the factory, Hedgy asked Tom how old his mother and father were.

He began to do some deep thinking. He thought that surely he should have a mother and father also. He began

88

to wonder where he had come from and who his mother and father might be. He went on thinking for days until one day he heard the little bird again. The bird was singing and told Hedgy that he must go and find his relatives.

"Where will I go?" thought Hedgy.

The bird said, "Follow me and I will take you."

Hedgy said he must tell his boss first that he was quitting his job, but added that he would meet the bird the next day. He went to the factory to find the manager, but as he approached, the man appeared to be frightened. In fact the whole factory was afraid of Hedgy, because of his great strength.

The boss started to shake with fear and asked Hedgy what he wanted. Hedgy told him he was leaving the factory and quitting his job. Tom knew that the other men would start to make fun of him again, now that his protector was leaving, and asked if he might go with him. Hedgy said he would be glad to have him come along. The manager told him he was welcome to stay longer if he liked, but Hedgy said he must go. He was paid first-class wages and given a gift of two horses, on which the boys began their journey, Hedgy taking his spear, and Tom his butcher knife. The bird was waiting for them and told them to follow him.

Hedgy's mother, still in the basement of her own home, was becoming very weak. The king and his family were all seated at the table having dinner one day, when a corner of the wall opened and in walked a skeleton. The skeleton took the guard, who was acting as king, by the hand and led him to the basement, to a room next to Hedgy's mother. Here he told him that since he had been so mean all his life, somebody was coming to kill him.

He said it was the son of the lady in the next room. After he said these words, he disappeared.

When the guard returned to the table his face was white. The family were out looking for him, so he called them to the table, but could not tell them what he had seen or what had happened. The skeleton was the spirit of his father.

The guard told them to bring the lady from the basement to have dinner with them. He asked her if she had any children. She began to cry and said she had a baby, but didn't know what happened to it, or even if it were still alive. She thought that wild animals had probably eaten the little boy long ago.

He then told her about her son coming to see them, and asked her to forgive him. She said she would, and asked him how he knew that her son lived. He told her that he had had a dream the night before.

He told them to dress the lady well—like a queen—because she was going to have company. He then had all his prisoners guard the city so that no one could enter the gates.

When the two boys, Tom and Hedgy, started to enter the city, the guards tried to fight them off. Hedgy fought with all his might and knocked one down after another. If they were not quite dead, Tom would take his butcher knife and punch them. More and more of the prisoners came, and Hedgy continued to kill one after another. The little bird stopped right in front of the palace and told Hedgy to enter. The king sank to his knees and asked Hedgy to kill him.

"Why should I kill you?" Hedgy asked.

He told Hedgy he was the real prince, and the queen was his mother. She asked how he knew this was her son.

90

She said she had a son at one time, but had put him under the hedges and left him there. Hedgy then pulled out the medal that the missionary had saved for him. When his mother saw this, she fainted and fell to the ground. After she regained consciousness, she kissed him many times.

The guard asked, "Is this really your son?"

She said that it was.

Hedgy asked about his father, and when the guard said he had killed him, Hedgy raised his spear, ready to do the same to him, but his mother told him not to, because she had forgiven him.

The guard promised, if his life were spared, to take his family and leave.

It was then that Hedgy began a new life with his mother and Tom. Hedgy's mother thought of getting new servants, since a number of the old ones had been killed when Hedgy tried to enter the city. Also, Hedgy decided to put new guards around the state. The first day when the servants prepared the table, they called Hedgy, his mother, and Tom. Hedgy was very much amazed. Nothing in his life was ever like this. At first he was so amazed he could hardly believe it, but as the days went by he got used to it. Tom had his own room at the palace, but he ate with them and was treated as if he were Hedgy's brother. The mother was very happy. Hedgy was glad to have found her, but was sorry that he never got to see his father. However, they all lived happily together.

After a month or two the people in the factory heard about Hedgy and were quite surprised. The factory was in West Virginia and at one time had belonged to King Jimmy. One day the queen and the two boys went to visit the factory, where Hedgy introduced his mother to the people. Everyone who had known Hedgy was glad to see him, but when the visitors left, no one could talk of anything but *Tom's* good luck.

A few years went by in this manner. Hedgy was perfectly satisfied to be living in the palace with his mother and thought of little else. Every day he and Tom would get their horses and go riding around the woods.

One beautiful day while they were out walking, they heard the bird again. The bird told Hedgy that he was to get married, but before he did so, he must find the magic rope and armor. He said that there were two brothers. One had the armor, which made anyone who wore it invisible, and the other had the rope, which was about two feet long and, when twisted, brought the possessor anything he desired.

Hedgy asked the bird where he could find these things. The bird told him to follow him and he would show him where they were. Hedgy asked how long it would take.

"About a week or two," the bird said.

Hedgy told him that he would go back and tell his mother about leaving, so the bird said, "When you get ready, meet me here in this same spot."

He went home and told his mother that he was going to leave for a while—he and Tom both. She was afraid that he would never come back and asked him not to go, but he refused to listen to her. His mother started to cry.

Hedgy said, "Why do you cry?"

She told him that she was afraid that someone would kill him. He told her that nobody could kill him—that only God could do that. His mother wanted to know why he thought this was so. He told her to get a sharp knife and to try to cut him. Of course, she had not known about

Hedgy washing himself in the blood. He told her to try and cut his finger.

She said, "I wouldn't do that for anything in the world."

He tried, and the knife would not cut. His mother then tried, but the knife would not even touch the skin. She said, "Maybe the knife just isn't sharp enough."

Hedgy told her to try it on a piece of wood. With one try, she cut it in two. He then told her how he had washed himself with the blood of the animal. His mother was happy to hear this.

The next day Hedgy and Tom left home. The bird was waiting for them. Before they saw it, they heard it singing, "Hedgy—Hedgy—Hedgy." Then the bird said, "Follow me."

They were now in the deep woods, where they found all kinds of animals—deer, lions, tigers, bears, wolves, and many others. Tom was afraid of them all, since most of them seemed to want to eat them. Hedgy had the spear in his hands and killed any animal that came near enough to attack them. He let Tom walk in front of him, and watched him as a father and mother might watch their own baby.

After a while they heard the bird say, "Here is a rock that is three feet wide and five feet high. This is where you must enter."

They looked around and saw many trees, large and small, but nothing else. The bird told them to wait there and watch the hole. "One little man will come out," he said, "and, when he does, grab him, and don't let loose until he gives you the rope."

Hedgy and Tom heard this and they both watched closely. Tom was afraid and looked all around every time the wind blew. He heard a little noise in the hole and thought that a rabbit might come out, but it was a little man, two feet tall. When Hedgy tried to grab him, he ran back in the hole under the big rock. Hedgy ran after him but could not catch him, since the little man hid from him. Hedgy could not see after he got inside because everything was dark. The man had two little girls and told them that Hedgy wanted the rope.

The little girls said, "Don't worry. He can't get the rope. Our uncle has a big hammer and he'll smash Hedgy on the head."

The girls asked their father if he had sent word to their uncle, and he said he had—with the magic rope.

When the uncle arrived he hit Hedgy on the head. Hedgy could not see him, because he had on the armor that made him invisible. The blow did not kill Hedgy. He stood still until he heard a voice saying, "He's still living." Then he swung his spear and killed the man in armor.

Hedgy took the armor and put it over his head. When he got the armor on, everything was light inside. He could see very clearly.

Tom was outside and could not see Hedgy. He was afraid and called, but no answer came. A lion was coming at him, and he was so frightened, he didn't know what to do. Finally he climbed a big tree. The lion came on, killed a horse, and began to eat it. Tom was in the tree, shaking like a leaf. The lion started to roar, and another one came. The second horse ran away before the lions got him. Tom was becoming more and more frightened. He was still in the tree, watching the lions eat the horse and wishing that Hedgy would come. Then an elephant came and stood under the tree. Suddenly he shook the tree by scratching his back. Tom prayed to God for Hedgy to come with his spear, so that he could kill the elephant.

Hedgy was still inside the rock cave. He saw an oil lamp hanging on the wall and two little girls who looked like babies. The little man sat and talked with the girls, who were embroidering, saying that Hedgy was probably dead by now. Hedgy didn't make any noise. He grabbed the little man by the head, so that he could not run away. When he was in this position, the man started to yell, "Let me loose! Let me loose!"

But Hedgy would not let him get away. He asked him for the rope. The man told Hedgy to let him loose, and he would give him the rope, but Hedgy said he would have to have the rope first.

He squeezed the little man much harder, and the dwarf pointed with his finger to the rope. Hedgy followed his directions to a little trunk, wrapped up in a dark brown cloth, and, on opening the trunk, found the rope, and a man appeared.

"What do you want?" asked the man.

Hedgy asked him how he'd got there. The man told him that he had called him, but Hedgy denied this.

The big man said, "Every time you bend the rope, I must come. You have the magic rope."

Hedgy told him to go away. He then took the oil lamp from the wall and put the little man with the hooked chin in its place. He took the little girls and went outside. He now had the armor, the rope, plus the two little girls. He didn't see Tom or the horses. He just saw the bones of the horse that had been killed. He called for Tom, but Tom would not answer. He heard the voice but was too frightened to speak, although Hedgy continued to call. Tom recognized his voice but would not come down, because Hedgy was still wearing the magic armor and couldn't be seen. When he took off the armor, Tom yelled to him and told him about the horses.

"Come on down," Hedgy said. "That's nothing."

When Tom was about halfway down the tree, Hedgy put the armor on again. He wanted to see if it were true that it made the wearer invisible. Tom looked all around but could not see Hedgy, so he started to climb the tree again.

Hedgy said, "Come down, Tom. Here I am." And he took off the armor again.

Tom could hardly believe it. "I never saw you," he said.

When Tom got to the ground, Hedgy put the armor back on again. Again Tom started to climb the tree. Hedgy pulled his leg, and Tom fainted. When he fainted, he fell from the tree. Hedgy took him in his arms and held him like a baby. Tom looked as if he were going to die, or were already dead. Hedgy tried to wake him up, but Tom would not move. When Hedgy could not do anything himself, he thought of the rope. He twisted it, and up came the big man. He had a dark face and was dressed like a clown in colors of red, white, and blue. He said, "What do you want?"

Hedgy said, "I want this man to come to life again."

The man stamped his foot and up came another man. This was the doctor. The doctor looked at Tom and could not find anything wrong. He gave him an injection in the arm, but Tom did not move. The doctor gave him another, and Tom opened his eyes. He looked at the two men and then grabbed Hedgy by the neck. He hugged him tight and asked him never to leave him. Hedgy said that he wouldn't. Tom wondered who the other men were, but did not ask.

Hedgy bent the rope again and told the men to leave. He told Tom to put the armor on, as he wanted to see what happened. He could not see Tom, but Tom could see him. He then told Tom they must be on their way. They had the two girls with them, who looked to be about a year or two old, but were much older. They were midgets. Tom played with them and laughed as if nothing had ever happened. When he got tired of playing with them, he asked Hedgy how they were going to travel without horses. Hedgy twisted the rope and the big man came again.

"I want some good, strong horses with saddles," Hedgy said.

As soon as he had finished the words, the horses were there, one for each man. On the back of one saddle was a satchel. Putting the girls with their embroidery in the satchel, they began their journey. After they had gone about a hundred feet, they heard the little bird singing. The bird told Hedgy that he must not go home yet—that he must get married first.

"Follow me," said the bird.

The day went by and it was getting dark. They stopped to rest and Tom and Hedgy talked, but the girls didn't say anything. Tom reminded Hedgy of the magic rope and armor.

"Why don't you twist the rope and make a good house for us?" he said.

Hedgy twisted the rope and the man appeared. Hedgy asked for good furniture and a home for them to stay for the night. The man then whistled and another man came and said, "What do you want?"

"Bring a house here."

Hedgy wanted to make sure it had nice furniture, but

Tom said that he didn't care about the furniture. All he wanted in it was something to eat. The house appeared and was like a hotel. In it was a huge room with servants. Tom invited the little girls to eat with them. They sat on high chairs.

After they finished eating, another man said, "Any time you want to sleep, here is the bedroom and here is the bathroom. If you need anything, press the button and I will be right there."

Later they all went to bed. When morning came, and they had checked to see that the girls were there, Tom played with them again as if they were babies. Hedgy asked Tom if he were ready to leave, and both went down to the dining room for breakfast. They then called the man to bring their horses, put the girls in the satchel, and began their journey. But first Hedgy twisted the rope and the house disappeared. After they had started, Tom asked Hedgy if he were sure they were going in the right direction. Just then they heard the bird say, "Follow me."

About six or seven o'clock it started to get dark. They saw a city ahead of them, and the bird told them to move when he moved. Again they stopped to rest, and Hedgy twisted the rope and called for food. The man appeared with four chairs and a table filled with all kinds of food. Tom seated the little girls and told them to eat. When they had all finished eating, it was much darker. They could barely see the lights ahead, as they waited for the bird. About ten 'oclock they heard him saying, "We must be on our way."

The bird went into the city, jumping from one house to another, and stopping on one big building. In front of the building was a sign that read "Hotel." On the street, there were many faces. The bird told them to go

98

in and rest for the night. He said the magic rope would tell them what to do from there. Then he disappeared.

Hedgy and Tom took three rooms, one for the two girls, and one for each of them. The porter showed them their rooms, and they went to bed for the night, but before Hedgy could go to sleep, he had to find out what he was to do. He twisted the rope, and the man appeared.

"What can I do for you?" he asked.

Hedgy asked what he was to do. The man said he didn't know but he would find out for him. He soon returned and told Hedgy that he was to dress in good clothes, and since he was a king, he was to wear a crown, which he would get for him. He gave Hedgy clothing suitable for a king, and told him to get up the next morning at about five o'clock, look out a certain window, and if anybody called, to answer. Then he disappeared.

Hedgy could not fall asleep, wondering who was going to be at the window in the morning.

At four o'clock he arose, dressed in king's clothes, and stood near the window. At about five o'clock a woman appeared from the other building. She looked at him and he looked at her. She said, "Good morning," and he said, "Good morning." Then she disappeared. The woman, who was a princess and sister of the king of that state, went into the next room of the palace and told her brother she had just seen a king. Her brother asked how she knew there was a king in the hotel.

She said, "I saw him with my own eyes."

He told her that she must be wrong, because a king would come to stay at the palace, if he ever came to the city. However, he sent messengers to see if there was a king in the hotel, but when they got there, they looked in the books and found no king registered. The princess still insisted that she had seen a king. Again the messengers were sent back to the hotel to ask who lived in a certain room. They went to the room and knocked on the door. Hedgy was still dressed as a king.

The messengers saluted him and told him that the king had sent for him. Hedgy told Tom to take care of the magic rope and armor, and went with the messengers to the king. The princess and the king were waiting for him. They asked him why he hadn't come to the palace instead of going to the hotel. Hedgy told them it was too late in the night when they arrived in the city. He said he was going to visit them later, but the king had sent for him before he got a chance. They asked him if anyone was with him, and he told them about Tom, saying that Tom was one of his best friends.

The king then sent for Tom also. The two messengers went for Tom and saluted him, just as they had saluted Hedgy. They put the two little girls in one satchel and the armor and rope in another. Tom carried the satchel with the magic things on one shoulder, and the one with the girls on the other. The messengers wanted to help, but he would not let them. When they arrived at the palace, the king asked where the two little girls came from. Hedgy said they had passed through a strange place, where all the people were midgets, and he had taken two little girls as souvenirs. He did not want to tell them of his experience. When they saw Hedgy's spear, they thought he was a very strong man. The princess asked him how he could carry such a big spear.

He told her that it was not heavy for him, so she asked her brother if he could handle it. He took it by the handle, but could not move it, because of the weight.

The princess said, "If you fought with him, what would you do?"

Her brother said, "There wouldn't be a fight. He would just get what he wanted."

Hedgy said, "I'm not so mean."

The time passed and an elaborate dinner was served. The king and his sister asked Hedgy and Tom to stay for the night and, when they said the would, added that they would be glad to have them stay as long as they liked. The princess liked Hedgy very much and wanted to marry him. The next day as they were talking, she asked him if he had a wife. He told her he had never been married, and asked her if she liked him. She didn't say yes or no, but made him understand that she did like him. Her brother told her that Hedgy was a good man, and if she wanted to marry him, it was all right. He didn't think that she could find a man quite like Hedgy anywhere. So the two were married.

After the wedding, when Tom and Hedgy went for a walk, they heard a little bird. They looked up in the sky and saw the bird turn into smoke. They stood watching it, as part of the smoke went to the left and part to the right. Tom was afraid, but Hedgy wasn't, as he saw the smoke turn into a statue, which looked more and more like a real man. He could see long hair and a long beard and clothing made from a lion's skin. He knew who it was and ran to kiss the statue, but could not reach it.

Then a voice said, "I'm sorry, but I can't take care of you any more. From now on you will take care of yourself."

When the statue said these words, he turned to smoke again, went higher into the air, and finally disappeared.

Tom asked Hedgy who it was, and Hedgy told him it was the man who had taken care of him since he was a little baby. This, as you have probably already guessed, was the missionary.

When Hedgy married the princess, his brother-in-law wanted to make him king of his own state, Massachusetts, but Hedgy took his wife and went back to West Virginia. He did not want to be king of another state. When his mother saw he was married, she was happy.

About two years later, King Henry of Massachusetts came to visit his sister and became acquainted with Hedgy's mother, during his stay of about a week. Three years afterward, the princess, who was now Queen Mary, went to visit her brother, King Henry, and all the family went along. He was happy to see them. They asked why he was still single.

He told them he had never seen a girl to suit him, but he knew of a princess from another state, Ohio, who had been changed into a marble statue by the curse of a witch. Before he could marry her, someone would have to set her free. Many people had tried, but every time they started to climb the mountain where the princess lived, they were struck by lightning and killed. Hedgy heard this and thought he might be able to get her for his brother-in-law, but his wife told him he was foolish to try, because it would be impossible.

They decided to try, however, and the next day Tom, Hedgy, and King Henry went to the mountain. Tom and the king started to the left, and Hedgy to the right. Every time Tom and King Henry began to climb the mountain, they could see the lightning start.

Hedgy remembered about his magic rope. He pulled it out and gave it a twist. Up came the man and asked

Hedgy what he wanted. Hedgy told him he wanted to be on top of the mountain and in the king's house, so the lighting would not touch him. No sooner had he said this than he was in the king's house. When he got there, he looked around him and saw a lot of statues, all made of marble. Some looked as if they were scrubbing, and some seemed to be cooking. All seemed to be doing something, but nobody was moving.

Tom and the king were still at the bottom of the hill. They were unable to find a place to climb.

Hedgy went from room to room, looking all around. Everything was marble. He saw a room that resembled a bedroom. The bed, chair, and even the mirrors had turned to marble, and in the bed lay a marble princess. He twisted the rope again, and the man asked what he wanted. He requested that the princess come to life. The man told him that he must kiss her right on the lips, and he must not miss. If he did, it would cost him his life. He, too, would turn into marble. Hedgy thought of his wife and children. He didn't want anything to happen to him, so he turned to leave. He went to the door and thought for a while. Then he twisted the rope again.

"Exactly where are her lips?" he asked the man.

"Right there." The man pointed with his fingers, but told him to remember that if he missed he would turn into marble.

Hedgy told him to mark the outline of her lips; then he kissed her and broke the spell. The household was back to normal at once, and all the lightning stopped. When the lightning stopped, the king of Massachusetts and Tom climbed the mountain. They figured that everything was all right by then.

The princess asked Hedgy to marry her, but he told her

he couldn't because he was already married. She told him that he had saved her and that whoever saved her must marry her. Then Hedgy told her he had saved her for his brother-in-law.

Hedgy introduced her to King Henry. When the princess saw him, she didn't like him and told him she would not marry him. It was now late at night and time for all of them to go to bed. Hedgy and Tom went to their rooms and left King Henry with the princess, who gave him a terrible whipping that left him black and blue. Then she went to sleep and he sat on a chair.

The next day everybody arose. Hedgy went to see his brother-in-law. When he saw him, he asked what had happened. King Henry said that the princess had just about killed him. He said she was stronger than he was, and there was nothing he could do about it.

The next night Hedgy told his brother-in-law to sleep with her, but King Henry was afraid. Hedgy told him he would help if she started to whip him again, and put on his armor and went along. When the princess started to whip King Henry, Hedgy gave her a slap and knocked her to the floor. She didn't know what had hit her. She went to bed and didn't move. King Henry didn't know what to do until he heard Hedgy say, "Go to bed with her." After everything was quiet, Hedgy went to bed too.

After this, it wasn't long before King Henry and the princess were married. Since the new wife didn't like her husband very much, they always quarreled and she told him he would have to kill his brother-in-law, Hedgy, before they could ever get along. He didn't want to do it, but he felt if this were the only way to get along with his wife, he must.

King Henry thought and thought about how he would

kill Hedgy. Finally he told a man if he would kill his brother-in-law, he would give him as much money as he wanted, but he warned him that he would be hard to kill. He said, "There is only one way to kill him. If you don't kill him with one stroke, he will kill you."

King Henry knew about Hedgy's washing himself in blood, and that the only way to kill him would be on this one white spot. But he knew it would be fatal for the person who tried and missed. The man asked him how he would know where the spot was, and King Henry told him he would mark the spot for him.

One day King Henry went to West Virginia to see his sister. He told her she should make a suit for her husband as a surprise, and embroider a blackberry leaf on his side, over the white spot. She agreed to do this and made the suit with the design as he had suggested. When Hedgy put it on, King Henry was happy and told the man to go to the spring and kill Hedgy, when he and Tom went there to water the horses that day. He said, "With one pinch on the blackberry leaf designed on his suit, you will kill him."

Hedgy and Tom saw the man coming, but paid no attention to him. Suddenly the man ran and stuck Hedgy with a knife and killed him. Tom ran with his horses to tell Hedgy's wife what had happened, and there was much sorrow in the home. Tom felt as if he had lost the whole world.

King Henry and the princess were very happy at Hedgy's death, and Tom resolved to find out just what had happened. He got the rope and twisted it; when the man came up, Tom told him that he wanted to know who killed Hedgy.

The man replied, "Pete Jordon killed him."

Tom asked that the man be brought to the palace; then he asked him why he had killed Hedgy. The man said that King Henry had requested that he be killed, and he had agreed to do the deed because he had a sick wife and many children to take care of. He said King Henry had paid him to kill Hedgy.

Tom went to Hedgy's wife and told her that her brother made the man kill her husband. Then she and Tom called Pete Jordon back and had him appear before the family, where he told the same story and said that he was sorry.

Tom wanted to kill King Henry, but felt Hedgy's sons should do it. After twisting the rope and requesting that they be given courage to do the deed, he took the two boys to see the king, giving one of them the armor and the other the rope.

The two boys killed the king and queen and returned to the palace. They told their mother what had happened. On the one hand, she was sorry because it was her own brother they had killed, but, on the other hand, she was happy because he had taken what she loved more than anything else in the world. She told Tom to take the place of King Henry in the state of Massachusetts; then she gave the rope and armor to her sons to have the rest of their lives.

# 24. The Bad Boy Who Became a Knight

A MAN HAD one son who was a very bad boy. He played hooky most of the time, robbed birds' nests, killed birds, and was mean generally. His father didn't know this, since around home the boy was fairly good. He thought his son went to school every day and was as good as the average boy, and when people told him he wasn't, he wouldn't believe them.

One day a fair came to town, and the father and son rode in to see it on one horse, with the boy sitting behind. He thumbed his nose and stuck out his tongue at the people who passed, until the father finally realized what he was doing. When they got home he gave him a hard whipping, and since he wasn't used to punishment, the boy was very angry. Soon after that, he stole bread, cheese, and money, and ran away. As he got farther from home, he came to a deep woods and couldn't find his way out.

When he had eaten the bread and cheese, he had no more food and was hungry, but didn't know what to do. Money wouldn't buy anything in the woods. Finally, he went to sleep and dreamed he was at the bottom of a pit, and his mother and father were reaching down, trying to help him. When he awoke next morning, an old man with whiskers down to his knees was standing over him. The man asked him why he was there and the boy told him all that had happened.

The old man took him home with him, gave him breakfast, and began to plan for his future. He asked about school, and the boy confessed he had gone as little as possible. The man said he must learn, and from then on, taught him himself, so that, as time passed, he was well informed in the things he should have learned at school.

The boy was glad to have food and shelter again, but he still didn't wash himself or say his prayers at night. Consequently, the old man told him what he expected him to do and how to do it; after that, he did as he was told. The man told him he could go in every room of the dwelling where they lived except one.

When the boy was twenty-one years old, the man told him he must find a job; that, so far, he'd eaten without work, but from then on, he must work. He said there was a king not far away who might need his help, since he kept a lot of sheep.

Then the man provided him with good clothing, and the youth went to the king to ask for a job. The king's daughter looked out and saw him coming, and thought he was a fine-looking young man. He got a job as sheep-herder.

There had been trouble for the sheep-watchers. Every one of those previously employed had disappeared. Evidently, each one had been killed, but no one knew just how or by what.

The old man had given the boy a music box, and every evening when he got ready to take the sheep back, he played his music box, and the sheep followed him two by two. The princess and king saw him from the window and remarked that he was like an officer leading an army.

There was a lot of black drapery everywhere, evidently in mourning, but the youth did not know what it was for. Sometimes he would take his sheep into the forest, where the old man was, and talk things over.

One day the old man asked him what news there was out in the world, and the youth told him about the black drapes. The foster-father told him that was in mourning for the victims of the dragon. For a long time, he said, a poor person had to be sacrificed from time to time, but now, it seemed, the people had to draw lots or numbers, and the lot had fallen to the princess. Whoever drew a certain number had to be the next sacrifice.

The man told him that at last he could go into the forbidden room, where, evidently, different suits of armor were stored, since the youth had made up his mind to fight the dragon.

The first day the old man provided him with a jetblack horse, matching black armor suitable for a knight, and a sword.

As a knight, the youth went to the king and told him not to send his daughter that day; then he went to fight the dragon in its mountain lair. But the dragon said he didn't want to fight that day—to come back the next.

The youth went back and told the old man, who said to go again the next morning. This time he rode a roan-colored horse, and wore a matching knight's uniform. Again he warned the princess not to go—but again the dragon said he would not fight that day

On the third day, the young man rode out on a white horse and a still different knight's uniform. This time it was snow-white, all glittering with jewels. He had talked with the old man before this third encounter, and the man had told him if he grew weak, to think about him and also his horse.

The third day the dragon was ready to fight, but it seemed to be a hopeless match. Each time the youth cut off one of the seven heads it would jump back with a burst of flame and grow back in place, more firmly entrenched than ever. Naturally the youth became weak and discouraged, and remembering the old man's words, he thought about the man and horse. Immediately everything seemed to change. Now, whenever he cut off one of the dragon's heads, the horse charged upon it, and kicked it 200 miles away. This went on until all the beast's heads were off and kicked faraway.

After the fight with the dragon, the knight was exhausted from exertion and loss of blood, and went to sleep. The princess, watching over him, had a doctor come and take care of him.

When he regained consciousness, he told the princess he had had a refreshing sleep, and she informed him he would not be alive if the doctor had not saved him. She slipped a ring on his finger.

When he was well enough to be out of the doctor's care, he went back to the old man in the forest, who told him he had still more things to do. When he went back to the palace to guard the sheep, he should bandage his ring finger as if it had been injured. There was to be a big celebration because of the dragon-slaying, and the old man told him he should take his music box and play it; if he were offered a present he was not to accept any money or valuables. He was to say that what he wanted was a glass of wine, to be shared with the princess.

When he went back the next day, playing his music box, he was offered a lot of money, but he wouldn't take it. He said all he wanted was a glass of wine to share with the princess. The king said this was an insult, since he was only a sheepherder, but the princess said, in honor of the dragon-slaying, they shouldn't deny anyone his wish. So, as the old man had told him, he drank the wine first, and then dropped the ring she had given him into the glass. When the princess was ready to drink, the ring went against her mouth, and she realized he was the dragon-slayer. She told the king he was the man who had killed the dragon, and they begged him to stay on at the palace. But he told them he could not do this—that he was a sheepherder and had work to do. Then he went back to the old man in the forest.

When he got back, the man said he must do one thing more. He must cut off his foster-father's head. The youth said he couldn't do this, but the old man said he must; that he had lived too long already—250 years—and had been a wicked man. He said his father had been a king, and he had killed his two brothers and then his father. While dying, the father had placed a curse upon him and said he would never forgive him until his heart was burned in flames. At the same moment, the palace or castle where they lived had sunk into the ground. Again the old man asked the youth to cut off his head and quarter his body, so that his heart could be burned in flames and he could go to his rest—and the young man did as he was told.

Following the old man's directions, the youth went to the place where the castle had sunk in the ground to fulfill his promise. When he had burned the heart, a voice from a bird spoke, saying, "Son, I forgive you"; he knew then the old man's soul was at rest.

At the same time the sunken castle and buildings rose up from the ground, and since the boy owned these, there was no need now for him to feel that he was not of equal rank with the princess. Preparations were made for a huge wedding with feasting and dancing. However, the boy told the princess he wanted to go home and see his parents first, so he did—in his dirty, sheepherding clothes, and his raggedest ones. The princess decided she, too, would visit throughout the realm and get to know her people.

The boy's parents were glad to see him, dirty or otherwise, but when they heard the princess coming, they hid him in an empty room. However, while she was talking to them, he yelled out, "I want to see that princess too."

So the princess asked to see him, much to the parents' embarrassment. But the embarrassment was not for long. Soon the boy excused himself long enough to dress up in his jeweled armor. Now he looked handsome in his fine armor, and his parents were proud of him. The boy told them that he and the princess were going to be married and that the old man had made him his heir. He said that he now had a castle finer than the king's, where he and the princess would live.

The parents and everyone for miles around were invited to the wedding, which was an unusually large one, with dancing, drinking, and feasting going on for days.

# 25. The Two Brothers

Two BROTHERS, John the younger and William the older, started out to seek adventure.

They walked along together until they came to a spring. There was a road leading to the right and another road went to the left of the spring.

William chose the right and John took the left. "Now when we come back homeward," said William, "and come to this spring—observe carefully the water in it. It is clear and so it shall be if all is well with us both, but if the water in the spring is blood, then death has befallen one of us."

They bade farewell to each other and on they walked. Soon William came to a forest, through which he wandered till night came on. He was tired, sleepy, and hungry. He made himself a bed and proceeded to build a fire. He took from his knapsack a piece of bacon and a piece of bread. He then took his penknife from his pocket and was about to cut a switch from a tree above him when he heard a weird sound.

"O-o-o-o-o I'm cold. O-o-o-o-o I'm cold," said the voice.

William looked up through the branches and beheld an old woman sitting there shaking and shivering.

"Well, if you're cold, come down and warm yourself," he said.

The old witch scrambled down and sat near the fire.

William went on getting ready his supper. He put a piece of bacon on the end of his stick, then held it over the flame. When the grease began to drip, he would hold it over his bread and let it drip on it.

"O-o-o-o-o I'm hungry," said the old witch. No sooner had she said this when off she scrambled to a nearby brook. She soon came back with frogs and lizards on a stick.

Seating herself near William she held her supper over the flame to roast just as William did. Still shaking and quivering, every once in a while she jostled her lizards and frogs against William's bacon.

William became angry. "Stop touching my bacon with your old frogs and lizards."

All in vain did he speak, for the old witch continued to shake and shiver and to hit William's bacon every now and then.

By now William was thoroughly disgusted, so he packed up his belongings and left the old woman sitting by the fire.

The old woman muttered a curse as William went out of sight.

He wandered on through the night. At dawn he arrived at a village. Although it was very early as yet, he could see people hurrying and scurrying about the streets. He stopped a man and asked him what was the matter.

"Oh," said he, "today at ten o'clock is the day the king's daughter is to be given to the dragon in the well unless someone dare try to destroy him. But no one will try because all the brave men who have tried have been killed. There are no brave ones left. You see, this is the only well in this village and if the princess is not delivered to the dragon, all the people will die of thirst, for the dragon will not permit us to get water."

The man then hurried on. William walked on slowly.

Every house had a black draping hung upon it. Every window, every porch showed signs of mourning. The nearer he came to the king's palace the blacker things appeared. This made William become braver and braver.

Up he walked to the king's door and announced himself as one wishing to tackle the monster.

The king himself fitted him with the best sword and shield in the kingdom. As a reward if he succeeded he promised him the hand of the princess.

Just before ten o'clock all the streets were cleared. Everyone was inside. Just as the clock struck ten, William walked up to the well. He heard a loud thundering sound. Up came the mighty, monstrous dragon. A fierce look came upon his face as he saw William before him instead of the beautiful princess. Immediately he began thrusting fierce blows left and right. William managed to dodge a few of them. Several times his sword struck the dragon, but to no avail. His missed every vital spot. The dragon was too much for poor William. Soon he was dead. The dragon left a note on the well stating that he would await the princess at ten, just a week from that day.

William was buried with all the reverence bestowed upon a brave knight.

John slept well during the first night. He arose early and continued his journey through the forest. It was now breakfast time, so he found a nice spot under a large tree, where he built a fire. With his penknife he cut a branch from the tree.

"O-o-o-o-o, I'm so cold. O-o-o-o-o, I'm so cold," said a weird voice above him.

"If you're cold, come down and warm yourself by my fire," said John.

Down came the old woman shivering and quivering,

wobbling and stumbling as she made her way to the fire.

She had no sooner sat down when up she scrambled and away she went to the brook. Soon she came back with lizards and frogs on a stick.

Seating herself beside John, she began roasting her breakfast. Many times did she flavor his bacon with lizards, but he said nothing. Once he moved over to give her more room, but never did he show signs of any anger, ill manners, or disgust.

Both John and the old witch feasted heartily. John finally told her he had to go on. The witch thought he was a fine young man and as a reward for his kindness she gave him a small gold whistle, telling him to blow it when he was in danger and needed help.

John thanked her kindly, then, putting the whistle in his pocket, he wandered on through the woods.

It was evening, and the sun had just dropped behind the hills, as John arrived at the village draped in black.

A man was coming toward him. John questioned him, asking the reason for the blackness in the village. The man explained with grief that the king's daughter was to be given to the dragon in the well in a few days unless some brave man could destroy the monster and so save the princess.

"Was there no man who would attempt to try to save her?" asked John.

"Yes, there have been many but all in vain. The dragon is fierce and mighty. Death befell all the brave ones."

"How do I get to the king's palace?" asked John.

"Straight ahead on that mournful hill."

Away hurried John. On arrival at the palace he was given good food and provided with plenty of rest for the

116

following days before the day for the duel with the dragon.

On that sad day, John was furnished with the best sword and shield that could be found. By ten o'clock everyone was off the streets except John, who arrived at the well just as the clock struck the last note.

A thundering sound roared out of the well. The great monster was before him. A fierce expression was on his hideous face as he saw John there instead of the beautiful princess.

Nearer and nearer he came, but John jumped and rushed behind him. Down came the sword, but not hard enough. The dragon became more furious, and sprang. Remembering his whistle, John quickly blew a shrill note that sounded through the village. Out of the woods came a giant lion.

"Roar!" went the lion. How surprised the dragon looked! Quick was John with his sword. Right under the dragon's neck went the shining blade. Red blood squirted everywhere. The lion sprang on the weakened dragon. Soon the monster was dead, and the lion returned to the woods. John went back to the palace tired, but happy that the princess was saved and the people would now have all the water they wanted.

Great was the joy and merriment throughout the village. All the black drapings were burned. The wedding ceremony was performed and all was well until John remembered his brother and longed to journey on.

He persuaded his beautiful wife to go with him to look for his brother.

On the morrow they started for the woods. A few days later they arrived at the spring at the fork of the road.

Alas! The water was not clear. Red blood was seeping

through the spring. John knew his brother had met death, so he and his wife went back home, where they lived a happy life together.


# 26. John and the Giants


THERE WAS a shoemaker boy by the name of John, who was not much good at shoemaking. A caravan came along, and a fellow had his shoes broken—needing fixing. When he got them fixed, he asked John what he charged, and John replied, "Four cents."

Just then a farmer came in selling cheese. John bought four cents' worth and put the cheese on the table with his tools.

Then another man came with broken shoes, and John had no time to eat the cheese. When he had finished the second man's shoes, John went to the cheese, and it was covered with flies. He took a piece of leather, hit the cheese with the leather, and then counted. Fifteen hundred flies he had killed! So he took a piece of ribbon and wrote on it: JOHN, STRONG MAN, WITH ONE SLAP KILLED 1500 MEN.

Then he put the ribbon around his head, walked around the city, and everyone looked at him and the sign.

John walked on and came to the royal palace. The king was having a war with the giants. His daughter was on the balcony and saw John with the sign around his head. "That's the man you want to kill giants," she said.

The king sent two guards to get John. John said, "What does he want?" He pointed to the sign and said, "See this sign? That's the kind of man I am."

John went along to the royal palace. He told the king, "Now, don't monkey around with me. I don't want any trouble. You see what kind of man I am."

The king told him he wanted him to fight giants. John refused. The king said, "You've got to go—on penalty of death."

John agreed to go.

He started to walk toward where the giants were, but came to a cherry tree with ripe cherries; he decided to climb the tree and eat his last meal. While he was eating cherries, a bird came around and John caught it in his hands and put it inside his shirt.

Then he saw three giants coming. One said, "I smell the little man. I'm going to have a good meal."

John pointed to the sign. The giants cooled off a little. They invited him to join them.

He said, "Don't mistreat me."

He joined them. The giants decided they wanted to try John out—see how strong he was—so they came to where there was a big pile of stones. Said, "Let's throw a stone—see who can throw it the farthest."

The giants took about a fifty-pound stone apiece and threw it. John put his hand in his shirt and took out the bird. The bird was scared, so he flew, and the more far he went, the more high he got.

The giants said, "He passed our stone."

They walked on and came close to the sea. They had

an iron ball that weighed about a hundred pounds, and decided to see who could throw it the farthest. John couldn't even lift it. He was weak. When it came his turn, he put one foot on the ball and yelled three times to tell them to look out over there.

The giants said, "What are you yelling about?"

John said he didn't want to kill anyone across the sea. So the giants said, "Well, never mind. We don't want to lose the ball."

They walked on and came to the giants' house. John asked, "Where am I going to sleep tonight?"

The giants said, "You sleep on the first floor, and we'll sleep on the second floor."

The giants held a conference about what to do with John. They were afraid of him. He was so strong. He had thrown the stone farther, and could have thrown the ball to the other side of the ocean.

The giants said, "We've got to find some way to kill him. If we don't, he'll kill us."

They decided to go down about the middle of the night with an iron bar and beat him to death. But John had heard all they said, so before they came down, he got out, put a log in his place, and crawled under the bed.

The giants came down with an iron bar and beat for about half an hour. A-bame! A-bame! Then they went back upstairs.

John got out from under the bed, took the log out, and went back to bed. The giants thought sure they'd killed him. Said, "He's finished now."

Next morning John was mad like a snake. Said to the giants, "My bed's full of bedbugs. Bit me all night!"

The giants said, "What you think of him? All that beating, and he claims bedbugs bit him."

The next night the giants held another conference and decided to cut a hole in the floor. They had lots of logs to burn and they decided to carry all these logs upstairs and throw them down on John's bed.

John braced his bed good and strong, and went under it again, because he had heard them talking. The giants dropped the logs and said, "Now he's finished."

After a while John got out from under the bed and yelled at the giants. Told them not to walk around. Said dust fell down in his eyes so he couldn't sleep. Said, if they didn't quit walking around, he'd kill all three of them.

They said John was certainly a strong man.

The next day they had to get the water. Each of the giants took a hundred-gallon barrel to get water, but John didn't want any. He asked for a rope, which the giants gave him.

Each of the giants filled up the hundred-gallon barrel, and John took the rope and started to put it around the well. The giants yelled at him and asked, "What are you doing?"

John said, 'I"m not going to fool around like you fellows. I'm going to bring the whole well."

The giants said, "Let it go. If you bring the whole well, it might leak out. Never mind. We'll carry the water."

Then the giants decided to try John at eating, to see who could eat the most. John started to worry. He took a walk—while the giants were making the mush—and found a sheepskin. He took his shirt off and tied the sheepskin around his waist and his neck. Then he put his shirt back on.

John ate all his mush. One giant said, "I've got indigestion."

John walked around and asked for a knife. When a

121

knife was brought, he cut his sheepskin and let the mush fall out. Then the giant asked for the knife and said, "Didn't that hurt you, John?"

"No, that didn't hurt."

So the giant took the knife and cut his stomach open and fell down dead. Only two giants were left, then.

The next day the giants said, "Let's go hunting, and when we see an animal or something, we'll motion."

Soon a turkey came along and lit on the giant's shoulder. The giant motioned and John shot—but he didn't shoot the turkey. He shot the giant. Now, there was just one giant left.

The giant said, "I'll give you three mules and load them up with gold—and you go home. I won't make any more war on your king."

John said, "All right, but no more war."

After John left, another giant came and, when he found what had happened, he said, "We'll overtake him and get the mules and gold back." So they went after him.

John looked back and saw the giants coming. He hid one mule and had two on the highway; then he stood with one foot up in the air and looked at the sky. The giant asked him why he was standing that way, and John said he had just kicked one of the mules, and he couldn't see it.

The giants said, "What would we do if he kicked us? He kicked one mule and he can't even see it."

The giants went back home, so John got the mule out, went back to the king, and married the princess.

# *27.* Smart Mrs. McCool

LONG, LONG AGO there lived a giant named Fin McCool. He was as tall as a house, and his ears were as big as pancakes. He was so strong he could pick up a bear and throw it like a ball.

Fin McCool was very big and strong, but he was afraid of one thing. He was afraid of a bigger giant named Cucullan. Not only was Cucullan bigger than Fin, but also he had a magic finger which made him stronger than Fin.

Cucullan had given every giant around a good beating —all except Fin McCool. He told everyone he was going to beat Fin too, just as soon as he could catch him.

One day Fin told his wife about Cucullan. Even though Mrs. McCool was so small she could sit in Fin's hat, she was not afraid of Cucullan. She told Fin that she would help him.

Mrs. McCool began to bake some cakes. In all the cakes except one, she put a stone. Fin was very puzzled; he could not see how this could help him against a giant with a magic finger.

Then Fin saw Cucullan coming. His wife told him to get into the baby's bed, for she planned to tell Cucullan that Fin was a baby.

Cucullan came to the door and asked if this was the home of Fin McCool. Mrs. McCool told him that this was Fin's house but that Fin had gone to look for the giant Cucullan, and she felt sorry for him. Cucullan couldn't understand this, so she started to show him how big and strong her baby was.

Mrs. McCool asked Cucullan to sit down and have a cake. The giant bit into the cake and broke a tooth on the stone that Fin's wife had baked in it. She then gave one of the cakes to the "baby"—the one without the stone. When the "baby" gobbled the cake right down, Cucullan was amazed.

Then Mrs. McCool asked Cucullan if he would like to feel the "baby's" teeth. When Cucullan put his fingers in Fin's mouth, Fin bit off the magic finger. ·

At this the giant Cucullan ran from the house screaming that if this baby was so big and strong, he didn't want to run into the father.

Fin climbed out of the baby bed, and he and his clever wife were never bothered by Cucullan again.

# 28. Lucky and the Giant

ONE DAY Lucky wanted to go fishing, but when he got to the river he could not believe his eyes. The river was gone. He ran all the way home to tell his father there was no river.

Because he was a farmer and needed the water to grow his crops, Lucky's father was concerned. He decided to trace the river to its source to see what was wrong. He followed the dry riverbed into the hills, and there in front of him was a lake made by the giant Elmo, who was wading in it.

Elmo looked down, saw Lucky's father, and told him that he wouldn't give back the river unless he could perform a task. The man agreed even though he knew that if he failed he would have to work for the giant for seven years. Elmo laughed and then put one foot on the hill and one in the valley.

He told Lucky's father that he must do the same—put one foot on the giant's land and one foot on his own land. The man admitted he could not do this, and the giant said he must work for him for seven years.

When Lucky's father did not come home that evening, the mother became worried and early the next morning started out to look for him. She soon came upon him working in Elmo's field. The giant offered her the same opportunity as he had her husband. She agreed, thinking the big fellow stupid-looking. Elmo posed the task of putting the same rock into two boxes at one time. The woman admitted she could not do this, so the giant said she must work for him for seven years.

When afternoon came and his parents did not come home, Lucky became worried and started to look for them. On his way, he picked up some things that he wished to save. When he got to the place where his father was working in the field and his mother in the kitchen, he told the owner he had come for his parents. The giant said that he must do tasks to free them. Lucky agreed, so the giant set him the task of standing with one foot on Elmo's land and one foot on Lucky's father's land.

This was no problem for Lucky since he happened to have some dirt from his father's land with him. Then the giant said that he must put a rock into two boxes at the same time. This was no problem for Lucky either, because he had a pebble and two small boxes with him, one large enough to contain the other.

These tasks freed Lucky's parents, but the river was still a prisoner of the giant. To free the river Lucky agreed to do one more task. This time he was to take out all the water from the lake with a spoon. This was no problem for Lucky either because he had a small spoon with him. Lucky took the spoon and began to dig at the base of the dirt wall holding the river back to form the lake. Soon the water began to trickle through, and the river was freed from the giant.

Now that the river was once again free, Lucky and his parents went home and were never again troubled by the giant, Elmo.

# 29. Mosquitoes

FARAWAY IN the mountainous region of Europe, there lived a man, his wife, and their son. One day, out of the mountains, came a maneating monster, who devoured the man and wife. The boy, Olaf, was away and was spared the same fate. When he returned and found that his parents had been killed and eaten, he swore vengeance upon the killer.

He began searching for the monster at once, but many years passed before he found him.

Olaf drew his sword and the battle began. He stabbed the creature many times, but could not kill him. The monster, seeing that he was losing, fled. Olaf knew he would have to find some other method of killing him.

He dug a large pit, put a plentiful supply of wood on the bottom, and then covered it up. When the monster came by, Olaf chased him toward the pit, and he fell in. Olaf then threw a burning torch into the pit and set the wood on fire.

Before the creature died of fumes and flames, he shouted to Olaf. He swore that even though he would be burned up he would not die. His ashes would go out in the world, blown by winds to the four corners of the earth, and these would be small, maneating creatures. This is how mosquitoes were brought onto earth.

# $\overline{VI}$

# Magic Objects, Elements, and Powers

# $30.$ The Ring

ONCE THERE lived a family of six people—the father, mother, and four children. When the father died, the mother and children were left to shift for themselves. The mother would make tablecloths, and John, the oldest boy, would deliver them on the days when he was not in school. They lived in a rented house and had very little for food.

One Saturday, when John had delivered a tablecloth and was on his way home, he saw some boys beating a dog. He begged the boys to leave the dog alone, but they paid no attention to him until he offered them the money he had received from the tablecloth. Then he was allowed to take the dog.

When he arrived home his mother asked for the money, but John told her he had lost it. The dog he had rescued was crippled and bloody. He said he had found the dog along the way.

After this, his mother made another tablecloth and asked John to deliver it, and not to lose the money. However, when John was coming back home, he met the same group of boys. This time they had a cat and were beating her to death. John again asked them to leave the cat alone, but they refused until John gave them the money which he had received from the tablecloth and took the cat in return. When he got home, his mother asked for the money, but John only told her the same story. His mother became very impatient and whipped him. After she had made another tablecloth, she told John to deliver it, and to make sure that he did not lose the money.

On his way back, he met the same group of boys. This time they were torturing a snake. Since John did not like to see animals treated in such a manner, he again asked the boys to leave the snake alone. But again they refused until John had given them the money he had received from the tablecloth. John was afraid to go home, for fear his mother would beat him. He began to run very fast and got very tired. After a while he stopped to rest under a tree. It wasn't long before he was fast asleep. All of a sudden he felt something over his body. When he awoke, he saw the snake that the boys had let loose. The snake dropped a ring which it had in its mouth on his lap. John looked at the ring and began to shine it, because he thought if he could sell the ring, he could get some money and give it to his mother for the three tablecloths.

When he started to clean it, a very old and ugly lady with buck teeth, her hair sticking straight up in the air, a big red nose and ugly face, appeared and looked at him. John was afraid and tried to run away, but could not move. So he shut his eyes. When he opened his eyes, he saw the old woman was gone, and began to run. Soon he was so tired that he had to rest again. Again, he started to clean the ring, still hoping that he might be able to sell it, and again the old lady appeared. This time he was not so afraid, and when the woman asked him what he wanted, he said, "Twenty dollars."

The old lady gave him twenty dollars and disappeared.

John was very happy. When he got home, he gave his mother the money, but did not tell her anything about the old lady or the ring. The next day he was still thinking about selling the ring, but, when he began to shine it, the old lady appeared again. Again he asked for twenty dollars and she asked him why he didn't ask for more so that she wouldn't have to come so often. John said, "I didn't call you."

But the old lady said, "Yes, you did. Every time you touch the ring, I must appear. I am under the command of the ring. Any time you want something just call me and I'll come."

Two or three days later, John bought a farm for his mother and the rest of the family to live on, and paid for it with the money he had received from the old lady. Two years later he got married and built a better home than the first one. The people could not figure this out. They began to suspect him of being a robber. One day while he was hunting, he left the ring at home for fear that he would lose it. Another fellow, who had read about the magic book and ring, wanted to get hold of the ring. The only thing he could think of was to go around and ask John's wife if she would like to trade any old gold for new.

John's wife knew that he had wanted to sell the ring when he first got it, so she thought that she would do well to sell it now, and get a new ring and surprise John. She picked the best ring out of the ones she saw and gave the fellow John's ring. When John arrived home, however, he became very angry because he knew that he could never find a ring like that one.

Because he was suspected of robbery, John was arrested by the police. The dog asked the cat what they were going to do, since they would not be able to get food from John. Since the dog and cat were witches, they spied on the fellow and knew who had the ring. They knew that he kept it in his mouth every night when he went to sleep. Since they were unable to get it from him, they called upon a rat. They told the rat that he must do them a favor. If he would do them this favor, he would never have to be afraid of any more cats or anything. Even his family would be protected for seven generations. They told the rat that he must get the ring from the man. The rat said that he would do it.

He went into the house and looked around all day long. When the man went to bed the rat noticed that he had taken the ring from his finger and put it in his mouth. After the man began to snore, the rat found some oil. He dipped his tail in it and then found some pepper and did likewise. He then walked backward with his tail in the air, being careful not to rub off the oil or pepper. He put his tail in the man's nose, and the man began to sneeze and dropped the ring on the floor. The rat then took the ring and ran outside where the cat and dog were waiting. They told the rat not to worry; that for seven generations he would not be bothered.

The dog and cat then brought the ring to the jail. John heard the cat mew and the dog bark, and asked the jail keeper to let him see his dog and cat for the last time. The cat came in, jumped on his lap, and gave him the ring. He squeezed the ring and the old woman appeared. John had one request and that was that he be allowed to go home to his wife.

When he got home, he found a lady in the kitchen, who told him that he had saved her life. John said that he could not see how he had saved her life when he had never seen her. She asked him who had given him the ring. John told her that a snake had given it to him, but she said, "No, it was I. *I* was the snake who gave you the ring." She told John that the boss of the witches had punished her and changed her into a snake. She told him if he had not tried to save her, she would have been killed. Then she told him to go to his wife.

And, as she said those words, she disappeared, and the cat and dog turned into real people. John thanked her, and thanked the dog and cat for all they had done.

# 31. The Three Brothers

A KING had three sons, and one day he called them in and told them he was going to die. He asked one of them to watch over his grave every night, after he was dead. Neither of the two older boys would take his turn, so the youngest watched for each of them, and then watched at his turn too. The first night, the father appeared from the grave, gave his youngest son a magic switch, and then went back into his grave. The second night he gave his son a ring, telling him that whatever he wanted, he could have. The third night, the father came from the grave again and said, "Son, you watch me?" And the son answered, "Yes, I'm not afraid."

That night the father gave him a magic horse. The youngest son didn't tell anybody about seeing his father or receiving the magic gifts.

There was another king, who had an only daughter, and the girl lived on a glass hill. All three brothers wanted to win this princess, but there was no way of getting up the glass mountain. The two older brothers tried two days in succession, sharpening the shoes of their horses' feet, but they did not succeed, and the king, the father of the girl, whipped them for even trying—both days.

The youngest son made three wishes. He wished for a golden pear, a golden apple, and a golden shoe, and, because of his magic gifts, he got them all.

Every day he rode a different colored horse—first a black one, then a roan one, and, on the third day, a white horse, and he wore a suit of white armor. He rode up the glass

mountain and gave the girl the things he had wished for
—the golden pear, the golden apple, and the golden shoe.

He was able to climb the glass mountain, even though
his older brothers were not, because of the magic horse
his father had given him. While he was with the princess,
she gave him a ring, and he gave her a ring in exchange,
but not the magic ring that his father had given him, of
course.

The princess liked the youngest son and liked the gifts
he had brought, which she showed to her father. The
king was surprised, as he did not know anyone had climbed
the mountain, but he was pleased with the presents and
said, "Who is this prince, who gives one golden shoe, one
golden apple, and one golden pear?"

And he said whoever it was could marry his daughter,
if he could find out who it was. So the youngest son went
to him, although he was dressed almost in rags. But he
seemed to have no shame about his clothing.

"Mr. King," he said, "I would like to marry the young
princess, your daughter."

But the king said, "Oh, go on. Get out of here! You're
dirty."

The youngest son said, "All right, I'm dirty. But I'm
good."

And the king said, "How are you good?"

Then the youngest son took the ring he had obtained
from the princess and threw it up the glass mountain to
her, and the princess called, "Father, that one! That's
the one!"

Then the youngest son dressed up in good clothing,
and the king had no further objections, so he and the
princess were married. And the two older brothers left
the country.

# 32. The Bewitched Princess

ONCE THERE was a young man who wanted to be married and have a home, but nobody would marry him, and he was so unhappy that he decided to hang himself. He took a rope, went to the woods, tied the rope to a high limb of a tree, made a loop, and was about to put the loop around his neck, when he heard a voice say, "Stop! Don't do that!"

He took the loop from his neck, looked around, but didn't see anything. So he said, "Well, something fooled me. I'm going to put the loop around my neck and go on with the job."

He put the loop back around his neck, when something called, "Wait, boy. Don't do that. Don't hang yourself."

He looked around again and didn't see anything. So he said, "This time I'm going to put the loop around my neck and go through with it. Nobody's going to fool me."

So he took the loop, put it around his neck, and again the voice called, "Stop! Don't hang yourself. I like you."

He took the loop from his neck, looked all around again, and at the foot of the tree lay a huge snake. The snake gave him some money and told him to go to the priest and make plans for a wedding. "Go to the priest and give him that money," she said. "I'm going to marry you."

While the young man was making the marriage arrangements, the priest asked, "What's the name of your wife-to-be?"

"I don't know," the man said. "She didn't tell me her name."

The priest said, "Oh well, I'll just give her the name of

Mary. Never mind." And he set down the name Mary.

When the young man returned to the woods, the snake asked, "What name did he give me?"

"Mary."

"That's the right name," she said. "That's my name, Mary."

This time the snake told the man to take as much money as he needed and get carpenters to build a fine building with 365 rooms. So the young man saw that the building was constructed and paid everything.

When he had finished all this, the snake said he should get a different kind of bird for each room, so he did. He went out and bought different kinds of birds—crows and all—and put a different kind in each room.

Then the snake told him to go to the butcher and tell him to have plenty of meat ready for a year's feasting, and the butcher agreed that he would. Then, with everyone invited for miles around, the wedding took place.

However, it was a strange wedding—with no bride present. When the man sat down at the table, he sat by himself. There was no woman with him. When he ate, he put one spoon in his mouth and another in his bosom. When he drank whiskey, he put the glass to his bosom and then to his mouth. And beer, the same way. Everyone wondered where the bride was.

When it was time for the wedding, they all went to the church and everyone said, "How is that fellow going to marry? He doesn't have a woman."

When the man came to the church, the priest looked at him and said, "Where's your intended wife?"

And the young man said, "No matter where she is, she is with me. So it makes no difference."

Just then a woman's hand reached from the man's bosom. The snake, which was wrapped around his waist so that it could be fed and not attract too much attention, had turned human for the time of the wedding. As a result, it had a natural hand to have the ring put on, so that the priest could read the ceremony. When the priest saw the woman's hand, he changed rings, went on with the ceremony, married them, and gave them his blessing. Then the man gave him some money and went home, and nobody saw the woman at all.

That night the man ate his supper as he had before. He put one bite of food in his bosom and one in his mouth, and fed the snake in that way. When it was time to go to sleep, the snake turned upside down, took off her skin, threw it under the bed, and turned into a beautiful young woman.

The mother of the young man and her daughter, the little flower girl, were looking in at the keyhole, as they were curious about the bride. When the little girl saw what had happened, she went to her mother, saying, "Mother, he's got a nice little woman—and she's awfully pretty. She took the snakeskin off, threw it on the floor, and turned into a woman. I saw it through the keyhole. What are you going to do about it?"

The mother said, "I'm going to watch my chance and do something to that snakeskin. I'm going to burn up that skin." And she did, about five or six nights later, when the young people were asleep.

The next day a number of wealthy people came to the wedding feast. One man was especially wealthy and owned all the woods around a certain section, so that he was very influential. He wanted to dance with the bride, but he was not respectful and made improper advances, so she slapped his face and told him to go home.

The wealthy man was angry at this lack of respect for his rank. "All right," he said, "since you are so smart, suppose that you clear off and clean up all that hill—some hundred acres of brush back of this dwelling—within the next twenty-four hours!"

The princess sent her husband and his mother to do the work at first, saying that the mother had burned up the skin, and now she must do the work—and she kept on dancing. When it came noontime, however, she was kind enough to take them their lunch. Then she sent the mother home, put her husband to sleep, and accomplished the task of clearing off the entire woods—cleaning up the great hill—by magic.

The next day the wealthy man came again. When he saw that the entire hill and all the woods had been cleared, he said, "You were smart enough to accomplish my first task, but you won't be able to do my second."

But the princess said, "Well, we shall see."

The wealthy man said, "Go down to the river, near the big rock quarry, and build a bridge across the river so that it will hang by one hair."

The wealthy man left again, and the princess told her mother-in-law and her husband to do the work for her. The young man started to build the bridge, working here and there, this way and that way, but he couldn't do anything. Then the princess came, brought them their lunch, sent them home, and built the bridge herself.

The wealthy man came back the next day, went out on the bridge, came to the middle, fell down into the river, and drowned.

138

And now that the wicked, wealthy man was dead, he had no more power, and the princess had no more worries. So the wedding festivities went on and on, as planned.

# 33. The Girl with No Hands

WHEN THE QUEEN of Persia was on her deathbed and knew she was going to die, she made the king promise that when he married again, it would be only to someone who looked exactly like her. After the queen's death, the king searched for three years to find someone who looked like his wife and then realized that his daughter was the image of her mother, so he determined to marry her. However, the daughter, rather than marry her own father, requested to be killed. As a result, the king made plans to have her put to death, asking that the excutioners bring back her tongue, an eye, and her hands as proof of her death.

When the executioners went to kill the girl, they were unable to do so, as the sword would not cut. Something held the sword back—evidently some magic to save her life—so that they couldn't chop her head off. Since they had to take back proof of her death, they decided to kill a large dog instead and take an eye and tongue from it, and the hands from the girl.

After the girl had sworn that she would never come back to her father's kingdom, the executioners took the proofs back to the king. Then the girl set out and traveled until she came to another country.

The king of this country had a golden pear tree, and something was taking the pears, but the guards could not seem to find out what it was, or to catch the thief. Many guards had been put to death for going to sleep on their jobs, and finally the king had set his sons to guarding the pear tree. The two older ones watched successively, but found nothing, since both of them went to sleep.

When it was the third son's turn to watch, he fixed up thorns for his head, so he wouldn't go to sleep and would see whatever was stealing the pears. He opened one eye and saw a vision in white. A woman came in and, when he asked whether she were a good or bad spirit, a voice said, "Good spirit."

He sat up then and saw it was a girl with no hands. Taking his overcoat, he covered up the girl and hid her. Then he went to his father and asked him if he would give him what he had found. The father agreed, and the boy told him he had found a girl without hands—and he wanted to marry her. The father consented—he said she could have artificial hands—so the young couple were married.

About this time the girl's father found out that she was not dead—that she had run away and the executioners had deceived him—and he was very angry. He had the executioners put to death and made war on the king who had rescued his daughter. In those days the kings actually fought each other, just as the regular soldiers did.

The king's son, the girl's husband, had to go off to fight in this war, and told his wife to be sure to use the seal whenever she wrote to him, so that he would know it was she. However, the stepmother, who was jealous of the girl,

found and stole the seal, and wrote letters, using the seal herself. She wrote a letter, pretending it was the son who had written it, used the seal and signed his name, urging that the father take the girl and burn her alive.

The king read the letter and thought it was from his son, but he did not want to burn the girl alive, so he made a dummy to look like her and burned it. He told the girl she had better go away—that there had been a plot against her life. So the girl thanked him and went away.

She passed a creek and saw a wild hog with only three legs—some hunter had evidently shot off one leg—run into the creek and come out with four legs. The creek evidently had some magic healing powers, so she decided to restore her hands, and she did. From that time on she had two good hands.

She was expecting a child, so it was hard for her to travel through the woods, but she kept going. Finally she came to a house with livestock on the place, but no one was there. She went in and stayed all night, and when a few days passed and nobody came she started to do the work and take care of the stock.

Her son was born, and when he was about three years old, some people came—the first people she had seen since she came there—two men, one of whom was rather elderly. They asked about the boy and she said he was fine, except that he wasn't baptized. So Saint Peter, for the two men were Saint Peter and Jesus, baptized him and gave him the name of Peter. When they started away, Saint Peter suggested that since He was godfather to the boy, Jesus should go back and tell the mother that when the child was twelve years old, he should ask something of God, and whatever he asked would be granted to him.

The king's son came home from the war and went to his wife's room, but she was gone. So he went to his father and said, "Where's my wife?"

The king replied, "You wrote a letter, telling me to burn her alive, and I did."

The boy didn't like this news, and when the king saw that he didn't, he told his son that he hadn't burned the girl—that she had gone back to wherever she came from.

The son started looking for his wife, with a large number of men to help him, but he couldn't find her.

Finally, when all the men had died of hardships but the prince and his valet, the two men came to the woman's cottage and decided it would be best to take turns sleeping.

The woman recognized her husband, but said nothing. While he was sleeping, the prince's hand fell down, and the mother told the boy to put his hands back under the cover. The boy did not want to do this, but the mother spanked him and he did. Later, something dropped from the prince's pocket and the mother asked the boy to put it back on the bed for him, and again had to spank him to get him to do it. The prince's guard watched over him, and when he awoke, told him what he had seen.

"You know," he said, "I believe that's your wife."

But the prince pointed out that this woman had real hands, and his wife didn't. The guard told him about the mother's spanking the boy to get him to do things—with her hands.

Afterward the prince came and sat down and asked questions of the boy's mother. The guard had said she looked like his wife, and she did.

The boy asked, "Mamma, what makes this red strip on your hands?"

The woman explained that the strip was there where her hands grew on. She said, "God gave me these hands."

Then the prince was convinced that it was his wife and asked how they could go home, since it had been such a perilous trip there, with so many deaths, and had taken so long. Of the whole regiment that had gone out in search of the wife, only these two had survived.

The wife said, "It will be easy going home. The boy will ask the good Lord and He'll give him what he asks."

The mother asked the boy—after telling him what she'd like, and the boy wanted it too—to ask the Lord for whatever he most wished, and his wish would be granted. The boy went out and whistled. He made the wish and also wished he could take his stable and cows with him. And, in about two minutes, they were back home.

However, the mother and the boy were concealed in a little house back of the palace.

The king asked his son what he thought should be done with the stepmother—what he was going to do to her—and the son said, "Nothing." He said it was the father's problem.

So the king asked the stepmother herself. He asked her what she thought should be done with a person who had done such things as causing an innocent person to be burned alive, and the stepmother suggested that such a person should be hitched to four horses and torn to pieces.

So that's what they did to her.

# 34. The Switch, the Tablecloth, and the Harmonica

THERE WERE three boys in a family. The father was dead, and the two older boys would go out to work on a farm. The older boys wanted the little boy to go out and work too, and he did. His big brothers whipped him, so the little boy started to cry and ran away from them.

He went into the woods and came to a place where three girls were asleep, with the sun shining right on their faces. The boy decided to get some brush to cover the girls' faces, so the sun wouldn't shine on them.

The girls awoke and said, "Little boy, what are you doing here?"

The boy said, "My brothers whipped me because I was late getting to work, so I ran away."

The girls said, "You're a nice boy."

Each one gave him something to protect himself. The first one gave him a switch and said, "Swing this switch and ask for whatever force you want. With enough soldiers, you can whip anybody—your brother, mother, or anybody else."

The second girl gave him a tablecloth. She said, "Whenever you're hungry, spread this tablecloth and any food you want will be delivered."

The third girl gave him a harmonica. She said, "Whenever you play, everyone will have to dance—even cows and horses."

The boy accepted this, too, and went back to his brothers. One brother said, "Now, I'm going to whip you again, for running off." The boy took out the switch and asked for ten soldiers to whip his brothers until they promised to do what was right by him.

After this, all three went home. The family was poor, and there was not much to eat, so the little boy told his mother he was going to fix the meal. He asked for a chicken for each one of them and a loaf of bread, and there it was. It appeared from nowhere, when he spread the tablecloth and asked.

They ate the good supper, but they were all worried. What had happened to the little boy?

Next morning, the boy got up and went to the king's palace. The princess, sitting on the balcony, saw the boy and said he was nice-looking.

The boy had done something, so the police arrested him and took him to the king. The princess was happy to see the boy; the king looked at him and asked how old he was.

The boy said, "Fourteen years."

The king said he wouldn't punish him—that he was too small. The princess, who was also fourteen years old, begged her father not to punish the boy. The boy said he was out looking for his fortune.

The king asked him to stay for dinner, but they prepared a poor table for him. The boy wouldn't eat, so the king asked him why.

The boy asked the king if he wanted a good dinner; then, taking his tablecloth, he asked for cake, wine, and everything else and invited all the royal family to eat with him.

After they had eaten, the king took the tablecloth away from the boy and wouldn't give it back.

The boy told him about the switch and called for a thousand soldiers. They were about to choke the king to death, so the king said, "All right. Here's your tablecloth."

The princess asked him to sleep there that night, but when the boy was asleep, the king sent his soldiers to take the switch and the tablecloth away from him, and they did. Then they put the boy in jail.

While he was in jail, lunchtime came, and the keepers fed poor food to the ones in jail, so the boy told them not to eat it. He said, "Don't eat that stuff. We're going to have a good meal."

When the sheriff saw that the prisoners wouldn't eat the food, he reported this to the king and said, "It might be that boy you caught."

So the king, queen, and princess came into the jail to see what was the matter. When the king came in, he put all the blame on the boy.

The boy said, "Give me back my switch and my tablecloth, or I'll kill you."

The king said that the switch and tablecloth wouldn't work for him as they did for the boy. He had asked for soldiers, but they hadn't come. He had asked for food, and it hadn't come.

The boy asked the king again to give back the tablecloth and switch, but the king said, "No." So the boy took out the harmonica and started to play it.

When he started to play, the king had to dance, the queen had to dance, the princess had to dance, the sheriff and all the prisoners, and everyone else.

The king couldn't stand it, but the boy wouldn't stop until he had the tablecloth. He told the king, unless he did the right thing, he would take his kingdom away from him.

So the king gave him back the switch too and said he could marry the princess—and he did.

# 35. The Bell of Justice

A SPANISH PRINCE had the misfortune to lose his eyesight. In order that his people might not be the worse for his loss, he hung a bell in his palace and decreed that anyone who had a wrong to be righted should pull the rope and ring the bell. When the bell rang, a judge would go down to hear the complaint and right the wrong.

It happened that a serpent had its home under the end of the bell rope. It hatched its young and one day when the little serpents could leave the palace, it led them out for fresh air. While they were gone, a toad took a fancy to the place, and would not go away when the serpent returned.

When the mother snake could not drive out the toad, it coiled its tail around the rope and rang the bell. The judge came down, but saw nobody and went back. Again the serpent rang the bell.

This time the judge looked around with great care and saw the serpent and the toad. He went back to the prince and told him what he had seen. The prince told the judge that the toad had to be in the wrong, and to go down, drive out the toad, kill it, and let the serpent have its home again.

All this was done. Not many days after, as the prince lay in his bed, the serpent entered the room and crawled toward the prince's bed. The servants were about to drive it out, but the prince forbade this. He felt that, because he had done the creature a favor, it would do him no harm.

The serpent glided up the bedpost. In its mouth was a precious stone which it laid on the prince's eyes. Then it slipped out of the room and was never seen again.

The moment the stone touched his eyes, the prince's eyesight was restored and he could see as well as any other man.

# 36. The Dough Prince

ONCE THERE was a princess who couldn't find a prince she could love, so she decided to make one. She mixed a dough and shaped it like a man, straight, tall, and very handsome. When the princess kissed him, he came to life. She taught him to talk and walk and he grew to be a fine young prince. They got married and she loved him more and more each day.

Because the bandits were causing a great deal of trouble in the country, the prince resolved to campaign against them, and in his pursuit followed them out of the country. This made the princess very sad because she didn't want him to leave.

The prince, after many months of traveling, fell in with these thieves at a palace where they were hiding out, in some far-off land. The queen of the palace fell in love with him and forced him to marry her.

In order to keep the prince from escaping she kept him drugged by giving him wine just before bedtime.

In the meantime, the princess-wife, who had been left behind, decided to go out and hunt for her prince. After traveling for several months, she stopped to rest, and while she was resting, a little old man approached her. He told her where she could find her prince and gave her three valuable stones. The little man told her to show the smallest stone first.

The princess went to the palace as the little man had directed, sat under a tree in the courtyard, and got out the smallest stone to examine. It glittered in the sunlight and caught the eye of the queen, who told one of her servants to bring the girl to her. When the princess was asked what she wanted for the stone, she asked to be allowed to sleep with the queen's husband one night. At first the queen got angry and slapped her face, but remembering that he would be drugged, she consented.

That night the princess did everything in her power to awaken him but she did not succeed. One of the servants overheard her and told her she would help her if she could.

The next day the princess again sat in the courtyard and got out the second stone. This one was brighter than the first and it also caught the queen's eye. The princess again asked to sleep one night with her husband and the stone would be hers. The queen consented, but the same thing happened as before: the prince did not wake up.

The next day the princess brought out her last stone and again the queen wanted it. The girl asked for the same favor, which was granted. This time the servant, who had promised to help, switched bottles and gave him plain wine instead of the drugged wine. That night the princess woke him up and he realized she was his princess. The servant helped them to escape and had horses ready for them.

The prince later told all he knew about the bandits and got the people to rebel against them. With the bandits out of the way, they all lived peaceably thereafter.

## 37. The Three Wishes

ONCE UPON A TIME there was an old man who lived with his wife in a forest, faraway from town. They lived on mushrooms, game, fish, vegetables from their garden, and fruit from their trees. They were happy and lived comfortably.

One pleasant June evening they were sitting in front of the house on a bench. Lightning bugs were flying about, some bright and some dim, but one was brighter than all the rest. At first it seemed faraway, but as they watched, it kept getting bigger and brighter every minute, until it was as big as an apple and as beautiful as a diamond. All at once it burst into a million pieces and lighted up the whole house, as if it were daytime. In fear, the old couple got up and started for the house.

"Where are you going?" a pleasant voice asked.

As they turned around, they saw a beautiful maiden, with a wand in her hand that sparkled with diamonds. "Don't be afraid," she said in a songlike voice.

"Who are you?" the old lady asked. "Are you an angel who has come to take one of us to heaven?"

"Oh, no," said the lovely girl. "I am a fairy princess

from the queen fairy, and I have come to fulfill three wishes for you within the next three days. Whatever you wish for in the next three days, you will receive. But be careful, and don't make a mistake."

As soon as she said this she disappeared, and nothing was left but the lightning bugs.

Surprised and excited, the old couple went into the house, not knowing what to wish. They hardly closed their eyes that night. The next day was much the same. All day long they thought, but could not decide what they would like best or wanted the most.

"I wonder if it would be all right if I would wish I had wings and could fly like a bird," the old man mused.

"Oh, no. Don't wish that. Some hunter might mistake you for an eagle and shoot you down. How would it be if I would wish to be young and pretty as I was when you married me?"

"Oh, no, dear!" the old man jumped up in protest. "How would that look—if you were young and I was old? What would people say? How could I go to church with you on Sunday? I want you just as you are now." And he kissed her tenderly.

The day passed and the evening came without any decision about their wishes. As the old lady was cooking supper by the fire, the old man sat beside her, his hand on her shoulder. "I don't know what I would do without you," he said. "You make such tasty meals."

"I wish I had a big piece of bologna," she said. "Then you would have a nice supper without having to wait for it."

As she said that, an unusually large bologna sausage slid down the chimney. In surprise, the old folks stared at the tasty meat.

"Look what you've done!" the old man cried. "Couldn't

152

you wish for something better than this chunk of meat?"

"Ah—I forgot," she cried.

"Such a stupid wish! Such absolute foolishness!" he said. "I wish the bologna would stick to your nose."

No sooner had he said this than the bologna jumped up and stuck to the astonished woman's nose and hung like a turkey gobbler's snout, only much bigger and heavier.

"Oh, pardon me, darling. I'm sorry. I forgot myself. What can we do now?"

"Take that thing off my nose," she cried.

He grabbed the end of it and started to pull, but the woman screamed out. "Don't pull! It hurts."

"What else can I do?"

"Take a knife and cut it off," she said.

He took his penknife from his pocket and started to cut the sausage, but she screamed again. "Ouch! Ouch! Stop! That hurts! Leave it alone."

They both cried over the mistakes they had made. She wouldn't be able to sleep with the big bologna dangling from her nose, and in the morning she couldn't wash her face. She couldn't do anything all day. "What'll we do?"

"Well, darling," he straightened up like a young boy, "we still have one more wish." His face shone with joy. "I wish the bologna would drop from your nose."

The instant he said this, the bologna dropped to the floor. Their faithful old dog grabbed it, pulled it off to the doghouse, and that was the end of the bologna.

After that, the old man and woman continued to live happily.

$$\overline{VII}$$

# Little People

## *38.* The Leprechauns

THE LEPRECHAUNS were leather workers and cobblers. Like all true Irishmen they liked liquor, horses, songs, parties, dances, and fighting. These little people all dressed pretty much alike. They wore loafer style shoes with large buckles, and long white hose. Their pants came down below their knees, and their jackets were of the swallow-tail style, with either silver or gold buttons. They all wore vests of some contrasting color with white ruffled shirts made from good Irish linen. The color of their suits was green, a protective color, probably selected to help the leprechauns avoid detection. They also wore high-crowned hats with turned-up brims and usually a feather.

154

It was indeed a known fact that any Irishman fortunate enough to catch a leprechaun was in luck for the rest of his life. To secure his release the leprechaun would grant his captor three wishes. It is hard to tell how much time has been spent by the Irish people in fruitless searches for the leprechauns.

Because the leprechauns loved music, dances, and parties, they would often come uninvited to Irish parties. Many a whiskey jug and punchbowl that became empty too quickly was credited to the leprechauns' love for liquor.

At one time or another every true Irishman has been made aware of the leprechaun. He has either heard music while in wild and lonely country, heard his little hammer, or missed something—usually liquor—that wasn't where it was supposed to be. The leprechauns did on rare occasions do good deeds for people. They would often make shoes for children in need, leaving them during the night for the child to find the next morning. At times, too, widows with hungry children have found gold pieces when their need was great.

Usually, though, the leprechauns had more time for pranks and tricks. They loved to hide burs in saddle blankets so that when the owner of the horse would get on the saddle the horse would pitch him off. It is said that many a poor Irishman has heard them laugh as he lay on the ground after such a trick.

Any unfortunate Irishman who insulted the leprechauns was indeed a sorry man. The leprechaun, if angered, could in the nighttime put a hump on a person's back or even change the luckless creature into a frog or a rat.

# 39. Peggy O'Leary and the Leprechauns

PEGGY O'LEARY was a young lass who lived in County Cork near the town of O'Dich. She was a charming girl, witty, and easy to look upon with her raven black hair, green eyes, and rosy complexion. Her mother was dead and Peggy was housekeeper for her father, Timothy, and two brothers, Pat and Mike.

She was wanting to marry with a young bogtrotter and peat merchant named Brian O'Neil. Her only difficulty was that her father and two brothers had no use for any O'Neil and even less than that for the one called Brian.

One sunny day Peggy went for a walk. She stopped by the brook to watch the trout jump for flies, and dozed off to sleep. While she slept two leprechauns appeared and were so taken by her beauty that they sat down and gazed upon her.

While she was sleeping, tears flowed from her closed eyes. This bothered the leprechauns and they decided to awaken her and find out the cause of her troubles.

Peggy told of the feud between her men folks and Brian and how she was unable to bring peace and have the wedding she and Brian wanted so much.

The leprechauns gave the matter some thought and then decided to assist her. They told her to be in the same spot the next day at the same time and they would give her what was needed to end the feud.

With that they disappeared. Peggy went home not knowing for sure that she had not been dreaming the whole thing, but certain that she would be in the same spot at the same time the next day.

The next day she was there and the two leprechauns came with a large vial of something that looked to be dust. They told her to bake a loaf of bread with the mixture in the vial. Then she was to divide the bread into four equal parts—one for her father, one for her brother Pat, one for her brother Mike, and one for Brian O'Neil. After this bread was eaten, her men would forget all their past differences and look upon each other with mutual love and respect.

This she did and the village of O'Dich saw the grandest wedding ever witnessed by Irish eyes, and they still talk of the grand music that was heard, but the source couldn't be seen. This was because the music was furnished by invisible leprechauns.

From that day until now the O'Learys and the O'Neils have been as one, thanks to the leprechauns.

# 40. Patrick O'Dea and the English

PATRICK O'DEA was as fun-loving a lad as ever walked the peat bogs. He liked fun and frolic, but had a very strong hatred for the king's troops, English soldiers, stationed in the village to maintain control for England. Patrick was constantly breaking English laws. This lawbreaking was very easy to do, as the English had made almost everything the Irish people liked to do unlawful.

Patrick was always either doing something or thinking of ways to torment the English. The English, in turn, had their own ideas about Patrick O'Dea. Their captain had often thought how nice it would be to catch Patrick and have the golden opportunity of seeing him on the gallows, hanging by his neck.

But even then, the English could not hang an Irishman unless they could show some good cause. Patrick was, in his way, careful at first. One trick after another he pulled, and his success made him careless.

One night Patrick went into the captain's quarters, borrowed the captain's spare uniform, and went to an English military ball in honor of a visiting English general.

Patrick did well and enjoyed the English food and liquor. He danced with their ladies and really had himself a fine time. But the liquor in his belly affected his brain and his quick wit. Before he realized it, the captain and several other soldiers were on to his act.

For a minute Patrick was sure all was lost. Then with a long hop and a big jump, he went through the window and landed running. With hue and cry the soldiers were after him. Patrick was just jumps away from the gallows the English captain wanted to decorate with him. Try as he would, he couldn't seem to shake his pursuers off his trail. He had indulged in too much fine food and drink and was slowing down, while the English seemed to be moving faster.

Patrick was twisting and dodging and trying to find some sort of a hideaway. Suddenly he heard weird music to his left. He rushed into a small clearing and fell flat on his face. His outstretched hands closed around two small objects that he knew must be—had to be—leprechauns.

Quickly he told them his troubles and requested their help. They, also being Irish, had great dislike for the English and made themselves and Patrick invisible. The English searched all over, but to no avail.

Patrick later appeared in another county, in the southern part of Ireland. He had to stay there until his friend, the English captain, was recalled to England.

Patrick took great delight in telling of his night at the English ball and of his help from the two leprechauns.

# 41. Don Mike O'Dolan

IN THE OLD DAYS, back in the time of my great-great-great-grandfather Donald Michael O'Dolan, the main form of entertainment was feuding and raiding among the different counties of Ireland. Don Mike, as he was called, was the chieftain over the O'Deas, O'Neils, McGilcuddys, O'Brians, McDonalds, and the McNeals.

His country was raided once by the combined forces of the O'Tooles, McGavins, Fluhartys, and O'Haras. This raid happened early one morning. Don Mike and his followers finally, after several hours of hard fighting, beat off the attack. But in the fighting, Don Mike suffered grievous wounds. A lesser man would have died where

he stood. His men carried him home and his good wife, Sheila, his friends, and relatives gathered around to do what could be done.

It was said in those days that when an important person was to die a coal-black coach pulled by six fog-gray horses, having a driver and footman dressed in gray, would come to carry the soul to its final judgment.

Sheila, who was Sheila O'Shea before she married, knew that her Don Mike was a prospective passenger for the death coach, so she took steps to keep it from arriving. The first night she had the men cut trees so that the road would be blocked at midnight. The next morning all the trees were out of the road in piles and the road was clearly open. That afternoon she had the men destroy the only bridge that led to their home. The next morning there was a new stone bridge that would be impossible to destroy in time.

Sheila was desperate and knew not what to do. Suddenly she remembered a tale told to her by her grandfather about a bracelet he gave her when she was a bride. He told her that he had once favored King Brian of the leprechauns with a barrel of his best Irish whiskey. King Brian liked it so well that he made Sheila's grandfather a present of a bracelet, telling him that he or his descendants could call King Brian any time by holding the bracelet next to his heart and saying, "King Brian, the O'Shea needs your help."

Sheila found the bracelet, called King Brian, and he came. Sheila told him her troubles, and King Brian immediately made the O'Dolan household invisible. The night when the coach of death appeared, it was unable to find the house and drove on by.

Don Mike, finally, with the help and loving care of

162

Sheila, recovered and lived a long and happy life. Every year on the anniversary of this date, Don Mike sent a barrel of his best Irish whiskey to King Brian.

# 42. Friendship of the Wee People

MANY YEARS AGO when my great-great-grandfather and grandmother were just getting their family started, they were having quite a hard time of it one winter. Their potato bin was almost empty, the cornmeal was almost gone, and they had one side of bacon left. In fact, they were just about to the point of having to beg.

One day an old woman came to the door and asked my grandmother if she could have some cornmeal. Grandmother asked her to come into the house, and told her that that they were low on their supply of meal, but what they had they would share with her. Then the old woman saw the bacon hanging above the fireplace and asked if she might have a bit. Again, Grandmother told her that this was their last side of bacon, but she was welcome to part of it.

The old lady took some of the cornmeal and part of the bacon, thanked my grandmother, and started to leave, but before she left, she told her benefactor that, since she had been so generous with her, even when the family desperately needed what little food she had, she would surely be rewarded. Grandmother said that a reward was not necessary and that she was only glad to help her out. The old woman said, "Ah, but the wee people are obliged."

Of course, Grandma told Grandpa, but he just smiled and said nothing. The next morning the cornmeal barrel was full, and so was the smokehouse. Grandma had indeed been rewarded.

# VIII

# Impossible Tasks and
# Friendly Counsel

*43.* Eleven Brothers and Eleven Sisters

THERE WERE eleven brothers who had only one sister. They decided they must go out in the world to find a fortune for her.

So they started out traveling, to see what they could find to give her a good dowry. They came to a castle that seemed to be empty. They didn't see anyone around, but they saw a table with eleven chairs. Eleven places were set, with an abundance of food, as if waiting for guests.

The eldest said, "How strange. Food, but nobody to eat it. Why shouldn't we?"

They ate the food and, being tired, looked around for a place to rest. They went to another room and saw eleven beds.

"Enough for us." And they all lay down but the youngest, who first knelt to pray.

"God, please forgive me, but I feel something strange here. Watch over us and protect us." He then lay down and went to sleep, too.

Near midnight, they were all awakened by music and saw eleven ladies approaching—all princesses and all dressed beautifully, in black.

"Who are you, and why are you here?" they asked.

"We are wandering over the world. There are eleven of us with one sister and we are going to find our sister's fortune, to give her a good dowry."

The ladies said, "There are eleven of us, and if you do what we want, it will go well with you."

Then they asked this and asked that, but nothing happened. At twelve o'clock they disappeared.

The next day, again the table was set with food—for breakfast, dinner, and supper. Everything was ready. That night the brothers went to bed as before. Near midnight, again a band played music and the lovely ladies appeared, begging them to dance with them.

The youngest brother warned, "Do not dance with them —not even one."

The brothers listened and again the ladies disappeared. The youngest of the eleven sisters came to the youngest brother and warned him. "You have refrained—held off from temptation for two nights—but it is on the third night the test will come."

The third night the ladies came to the brothers again

and lay down beside them. The youngest brother, being a God-fearing man, warned his brothers to leave them alone.

"Do not even think evil," he said. "Refrain from touching them."

The ladies lay down beside the men, and the older brothers whispered among themselves. "What does our youngest brother know? He is so young and innocent. We do not have to do as he says."

This thought had no more than passed through their minds when the ladies disappeared into nothingness. Ten of the brothers, the ones who had thought evil, turned to stone—stiff as posts in their beds. The youngest brother saw this and felt strange. The youngest sister came to him and said, "If you want me, you will have to go out in the world and find me."

So the youngest brother went out, hunting for the princess. He went here and there. In one place, near a cave, stood a big man, a giant, who said to the boy, "Where are you going, Little Man?"

"I am hunting for a princess. How can I find her?"

And the giant replied, "There is a princess in this cave."

The youngest brother went into the cave and searched all over, but did not find her.

"Did you see anything?" asked the giant.

"Nothing except a big pile of gold."

"You may go and help yourself to the gold."

"How can I carry it? It's of no use to me."

"Well, come and I'll help you. Get on my back and I'll carry you—and we will go together."

They came to a place where they saw a very fat man—big like a barrel.

"Where are you going?" the giant asked him.

"Where am I going? Well, I am just wandering over the world. And you?"

"We are wanderers too. Why not come with us and be our friend?"

They went along together and met another man whose eyes were blindfolded. They asked him why he went around with his eyes covered.

He replied. "If my eyes were not tied up and I looked on a stone, it would turn to powder."

The youngest brother said, "Since you see so well to get around with your eyes blindfolded, perhaps you will be good enough to tell me where my princess is hiding. You could see."

The blindfolded man, who was called Sharp Eyes, looked about him and into the distance, far, far away. Then he said, "Oh, she is far away—in a strange castle. I see ten others with her—imprisoned in a glass castle."

The younger brother turned to the giant. "Do you think you could carry us all on the journey to the castle where the princess is?"

The giant nodded. "Oh, yes. I can easily carry you all. Get on my back."

So he gathered up the youngest brother, the fat man, and the blindfolded man on his back, and took such long steps that he covered a mile at a step. They covered much ground, but night fell, so they had to rest and sleep.

There came to them a little, withered old man, and they asked him how to get to the castle. He shook his head.

"There is nothing you can do to get into that castle. Everyone who ever tried disappeared and was never heard of again. Everything that is taken in is never seen again."

The fat man said, "Show me how to get there." I will

blow myself up and stand guard in the doorway, so that not even an ant can pass me."

The giant said, "And I will stand over the roof of the castle. Whoever goes in or out, I can see him."

Sharp Eyes, the blindfolded man, said, "Humph! If I look at him, he'll turn to dust."

The eleven princesses were in the glassed-in castle and sat around talking and laughing. They could be seen, but could not get out. They were like pictures, in that they could not talk back, and they seemed to be holding pictures. The youngest brother saw his princess, the youngest one, there, with the others.

The old man warned them all not to touch the princesses. The eleven brothers—all but the youngest—were still like stone in a faraway castle, but the princesses seemed to have found pictures of all of them. Each princess held and smiled at the picture of the brother of her choice.

The next day the youngest brother said, "I cannot see the youngest princess." He turned to the giant. "You were standing over the roof of the castle. Did you see where she went?"

"No," said the giant.

The youngest brother was disappointed and angry. "You don't know anything and can't *do* anything!" he said.

"Wait a minute," Sharp Eyes said, "I will look. Unbind my eyes. I will see where she is."

So they untied his eyes and he looked and looked, and far away in the woods he saw a dove. He told the youngest brother he must go and get it and return before sunrise.

The youngest brother turned to the giant. "Will you take me there?"

"Of course," said the giant. "Get on my back and away we'll go."

The youngest brother got on the giant's back, and the giant took big, long steps—one, two, three, and they were in the woods. The youngest brother grabbed the dove and they rushed back, with the dove in his arms.

Next day the watchman, the good giant, said to the youngest brother, "Didn't you bring back the dove? Is everything there—?"

"Yes, I did," said the youngest brother.

Then he saw his princess in the castle, dressed in white to the waist, as all the other princesses were. Up until this time they had all been dressed in black.

"One night has gone well," the youngest princess said. "Now another night is to go by."

During the day the princess again disappeared. Sharp Eyes looked for her again and saw her turned into a stone, tiny as a grain of rice. The good giant again took the youngest brother and Sharp Eyes on his back and they went to get this small stone, which was the princess. They had to get back before sunrise, and did, after which they let her go.

When they saw the princess in person, she and her sisters were dressed in white to their knees. The third day she disappeared again. The youngest brother appealed to Sharp Eyes.

"Will you help me look for her again?"

Sharp Eyes said, "I am looking and looking, but I don't see her."

"We must find her before sunrise," the youngest brother said. "If we don't find her we will all become prisoners."

Sharp Eyes looked and looked hard—and saw the princess now turned into a fish in a lake. The youngest brother turned to the fat man.

171

"You can hold so much—you come with us and drink the water out of the lake so I can catch the fish."

The good giant took them on his back and they went to the lake. The fat man drank and drank and drank—until they saw the little princess-fish. The youngest brother caught the fish, brought it back, and it turned into the princess again. All the eleven princesses were in white now. They had been freed from a curse that had been put on them.

"We thank you for freeing us," they said to the youngest brother.

The youngest princess said, "Go to the eleventh bed, my bed, in the castle where the brothers are. Under that bed is a well. Get some water out of it and sprinkle it over your brothers, because I have no right to do it."

So the youngest brother went to the castle where his brothers were, got some water from the well, sprinkled it over them, and they were all revived to life.

The princes and princesses all got married, and a husband was found for the sister, so that there were twelve couples to dance at the wedding. The fat man danced at the wedding too, and the water in his stomach went boom—boom—boom—like a huge drum as he danced.

What happened to Sharp Eyes? He is in America now, a trick auto driver. He can steer a car, blindfolded, between some tiny balls. As for Long Legs, the good giant, he is a watchman now, and always will be.

# 44. The Ax, the Spade, and the Walnut

ONCE THERE was a man who had three sons. He was very poor, but he owned a farm. In his only pasture, the farmer had broken his back, digging out boulders. Because he was poor, he sent his three sons, Peter, John, and Louie, out into the world to seek their fortunes.

Peter and John decided to go to the king's castle, because against the castle a great oak had grown up that shut out all the light. No one had been able to cut it down. The king said he would give a rich treasure to anyone who could cut the tree down, but, so far, no one was able to do so. The castle, built on a high hill, had no water well. The king offered double the treasure to anyone who could dig a well filled with water. So Peter, John, and Louie set out.

They had not gone far before they came to a thick forest. In the distance they heard a chopping sound. Louie, being a curious type of boy, went to see what it was, while his brothers waited under a tree. He followed the sound, on and on, wandering through the trees until he came to a clearing where an ax was chopping, all by itself. The ax told him that it had been waiting for him. Louie took off the handle and put the blade in his pouch, after which he went back to his brothers and they went on.

They had not gone far when they came to a steep ledge of rock, and at the top, they heard a digging sound. Peter and John wanted to go on but Louie had to see what it was. He climbed up the cliff and when he got to the top, he saw a spade digging all by itself. The spade told him it had been waiting for him a long time. Louie, again, took the spade from the handle and put it in his pouch. He rejoined his brothers and on they went.

After they had traveled some distance, they stopped at a little stream. Louie wondered where the water came from. He decided to follow the stream, while his brothers cooled themselves in the shade. Although it was a long distance, he finally found a walnut, from which the water was coming. The walnut also told him it had been waiting for him. Louie plugged the hole in the walnut and put it in his pouch. He rejoined his brothers and they traveled on.

It was not long before they came to the castle. Many people had tried to cut the tree down, but no one had succeeded, and the tree kept growing larger. The king now offered half the kingdom and the princess for his wife to anyone who could accomplish the task. First Peter tried to cut down the tree, but failed. Then John tried and failed. Then it was Louie's turn. He put the handle on the ax and told it to cut down the tree, and it did. He then put the handle on the spade and told it to dig a well, which was done. He then unplugged the walnut and placed it in the well and the water filled it.

The king was so pleased that he gave Louie half the kingdom and the princess for his wife, just as he had promised.

# 45. The Golden Duck

THE KING had a tree with golden apples, and something was taking the apples, but he couldn't find out what it was. He had guards to watch, but because they couldn't catch the thief he had them put to death or imprisoned.

The king had three sons, and everyone thought the youngest one was not as smart as his brothers. However, when no one else could catch the thief, he kept watch on this tree and found it was a golden duck that was taking the apples. He caught the duck, but it got away, leaving two feathers.

The next morning he took these feathers to the king, his father, and told him what had happened. The king said someone would have to look for the duck—and find it —wherever it was.

So the two older brothers got ready, packed a lunch, and started out to look for the golden duck. No one had much confidence in the ability of the youngest son, since he never had much to say for himself—partly because his brothers never gave him a chance; consequently, he was left at home.

The two brothers went on until they came to a hotel with the sign: TODAY YOU PAY—TOMORROW FOR NOTHING.

This sounded like a good thing, but one must realize that when tomorrow comes, it is today. In other words, one paid every day.

The two brothers went into the hotel and started to drink, play cards, make love to the girls, and have a good time generally. They had the best of meals and kept drinking and playing cards until they had spent all their money.

When their money was gone, the hotelkeeper said, "Since you have no money to pay your bill, I'll have to put you in jail and keep you there for a year." And he did.

A year passed and the two brothers didn't come back, so the youngest son went to the king and said he would go. The king hated to see him leave, since the other boys hadn't come back, and he was his last son, but he finally agreed to let him go. So the boy got an old plug horse that looked like a scarecrow, took a little bit of money, started out, and came to the same hotel.

He, too, saw the sign that said: TODAY YOU PAY—TOMORROW FOR NOTHING, but he didn't spend all his money the first night. He ate a little, drank a little, and slept a little—not much. He didn't even take a room—just slept on a bench, with his horse outside. Nobody bothered him because he looked poor.

When nighttime came, the hotelkeeper opened up the chimney and picked up an old, black man—someone who had not paid his bill and had been put in the chimney and smoked black.

After a while the youngest son said, "Why did you pick up this old man, and why is he black? What happened to him?"

And the hotelkeeper said, "I've been smoking him up for seven years. I'm going to smoke him up for seven more years. Fourteen years I'm going to smoke him up." He went on to explain that the man owed him money and didn't pay.

"How much did he owe?" the youngest brother asked.

The hotelkeeper told him and the young man pulled

out his money and paid him. Then he said, "Now, give me the man's body."

The hotelkeeper did this and the youth took the body to the woods, dug a hole, and buried it. Then he started back to the hotel, but the dead man called, "Wait a little bit."

Arising from the grave, the dead man came up to the young man and said, "Thank you very much for rescuing me and giving me a proper burial. I'm going to do you a favor for this—anything you want."

And the boy said, "Well, that's fine."

Then he went back to the hotel, drank some coffee, and ate a little food; the next day he started on his journey to find the golden duck.

Soon after he left the hotel, the dead man came up to him and said, "You need a good horse, so I'll turn into one. Would you like me to be a gray horse?"

"Yes," the boy said.

"How would you like to travel? Would you rather I would fly in the air or gallop along the ground?"

The boy said, "I'd like for you to take me wherever I have to go as fast as possible, but I'd rather you'd keep on the ground."

They started out, the dead man and the boy, as a horse and rider, and traveled until they came to the palace where the golden duck was.

They stopped and the dead man said, "I'll go over across the road and turn into a stump, and when you're ready to leave, come over and pound on the stump with your switch. In the meantime, you go inside and get the golden duck, but do not take the gate that it's sitting on. Open the gate, but leave it there. Go into a hall and you will see a

177

lot of people, all asleep, on guard, so that no one can take the golden duck. Pay no attention to them. Just catch the duck and bring it here, and you'll have no trouble. But don't take anything but the duck.

The boy went into the hall and saw a lot of people, all asleep, and outside, he saw the golden duck, sitting on the gate. The boy looked at the gate, and it was so nice, so artistically made, that he could not resist taking it along too. When he did, the duck cried out, "Help! Somebody is stealing me!"

By that time the guards all awoke and the servants in the kitchen came out, and the boy was caught. Then the king came out and said, "Well, you're smart. You came here and caught the golden duck all alone. I'll tell you what I'll do. In the next town, there is a horse with a golden tail and a golden mane. He's a beautiful, high-spirited horse, and if you can bring me that horse, I'll give you the golden duck."

The boy left and went over and pounded on the stump, to tell his friend what had happened.

The dead man arose, turned back into a horse and said, "I told you not to take the gate. The king caught you while you were taking the gate. But I'll help you again. Sit down here, and I'll tell you what to do, and this time do as I tell you. Take the horse outside, and you will be safe. But if you take the bridle, the king who owns the horse will catch you."

It was the same thing again. The boy saw the horse, jumping and neighing, a beautiful horse with a golden tail and mane. On the horse was a costly bridle of gold, set with all kinds of stones—diamonds and every other kind.

He thought to himself, "That's too pretty to leave here.

178

I'm going to take the bridle too. I'll catch the horse and leave the bridle on it."

Again the boy was caught. The king who owned the horse caught him and said he was going to kill him.

"But," he explained, "I am not going to kill you in the ordinary way. In the next town, there is a girl with golden hair, a princess. If you will bring me this girl, I'll give you the horse, but you'll probably lose your life in trying to do this."

The boy went back to the gray horse, and they started on their journey after the princess with the golden hair. When they were almost there the dead-man helper, the gray horse, spoke.

"Listen," he said. "When the girl with the golden hair comes down, she will want to kiss and hug you, but don't let her. Slap her as hard as you can on the mouth, then take her hand and go outside. Nobody will bother you if you do as I say."

Then he pointed to a picket fence with high stakes. "Do you see that fence of sharp stakes over there? Every stake has a dead man's head on it—all but one. That one is for you. These heads are men who have tried to win the princess with the golden hair but have failed. You had better listen to me this time. This is the last time I am going to help you."

The boy went inside and saw a lot of people in a large hall. Everyone was sitting down, but nobody said anything. The girl with the golden hair came in and started to put her arms around him, but he slapped her on the mouth, took her hand, and went out where the stump was.

The stump, now a gray horse again, said, "All right. Sit down."

The girl said, "Thank you. You have made me well."

The boy sat down by the horse. The next thing was to get the horse with the golden tail from the second king. The horse, the dead-man helper, spoke to the boy.

"Listen," he said, "when we get almost there, you stay with the girl for a while. I'll make another girl, exactly like this one, and you can deliver her to the king and get the magic horse."

So that is what they did. Soon after their arrival, a second girl appeared that looked just like the princess with the golden hair. The boy took this girl to the king, who said, "I'm glad," and gave him in return the magic horse and bridle. However, although the girl looked just like the real princess, when she started to kiss the king, she turned into a bear and jumped at him. The boy, the princess, and the dead-man helper rode away with the magic horse and bridle. When they reached the palace of the first king, where the golden duck was, the dead man spoke again.

"I'm going to turn into a horse with a golden tail and mane and jeweled bridle just like this one, and you deliver that horse and get the golden duck. And, after you have the golden duck, take the girl, horse, and duck and go— don't wait for anything."

So the boy did this. He delivered the horse and bridle to the king, who gave him the golden duck and the gate.

The king was well-pleased with the horse, which was exactly like the real one, with a golden tail and mane, and which jumped and neighed continually. However, when two dogs passed, chasing a rabbit, the horse turned into an owl and flew into the woods. The king was terribly disappointed and said, "Now I've lost everything!"

When the dead man came back, he said to the boy, "Now you have the golden duck, the horse with the golden tail and mane, and the princess with the golden hair, but you still have to be on the lookout for trouble. When you come to the next road, you will see a black man like me, who will try to sell you a pair of shoes, but you must not buy them. Later a beggar will ask for a piece of bread or something to eat, but you must not give him anything. Keep traveling, and you will come to a place where there is a crowd of people, but you must not go there or even stop. If you do, that will be the end of you."

Then the dead man brought a nice saddle and blanket for the magic horse, and the boy and girl rode off with the golden duck. On the road, a black man stopped them and wanted to sell them a pair of shoes.

"You have a nice, pretty girl," he said. "Why don't you buy a pair of nice shoes for her?"

But the girl said, "No, don't buy me any shoes. Remember what that man told you. Don't buy anything."

So they went on. Soon a beggar came, asking for a crust of bread.

"Please," he said, "I'm hungry. Give me a little piece of bread."

But the boy said, "No, I have nothing to give you."

Soon he came to the hotel where he had spent the night and left his old horse. He looked for his horse, but couldn't find it. He looked up on the hill and saw a crowd of people, and wanted to go up there.

But the girl said, "You remember what that man told you. If you go up there where all those people are, you may be killed."

But he went anyway. When he got to the top of the

hill, he saw that a crowd of people had gathered to watch the hanging of two men, and that the men were his two brothers.

When he saw that his two brothers were about to be hanged, and found out that it was for debts they owed— they's been drinking, playing cards, and having a good time generally all this time—he asked how much they owed and paid their debts. Then he started home again, taking his two brothers with him.

On the way one of the brothers said to the other, "What will we do? This boy will tell Father everything, and he'll have us put to death probably. We'd better think of a way to do away with him first, somehow."

The other brother said, "Yes, but how can you do that?"

The first brother said, "Not far from here, there's a well, and when we stop for a drink of water and he goes to draw up the water, I'll push him in the well. And we'll make the girl swear not to tell anybody anything about it."

The other brother agreed to this, and when they stopped for a drink and the youngest brother started to pull up the water, the oldest brother pushed him in, and he fell to the bottom of the well.

When the brothers asked the girl to swear not to say anything about it to anyone, she said, "All right. I'll swear for a year and six Sundays. If, in that time, the youngest brother doesn't come back, I'll marry someone else. But until that time, I won't marry anyone."

They went on home then, the two brothers, taking with them the girl, the horse, and the golden duck. But the girl never laughed or even smiled, and the duck never made any noise at all, and the horse acted as if he were dead.

In the meantime the youngest brother was still alive at

the bottom of the well. It was a deep well, and he couldn't get out. A year passed, and all this time an eagle had carried him something to eat every day.

Finally the eagle spoke to him and said, "Listen, try to catch hold of my spoon down there. I'm going to try to take you outside. I'd like to carry you out."

But the boy said, "Oh, no. You're small. You couldn't carry me."

And the eagle said, "I've got lots of power. I'm going to pull you up."

After he'd pulled him out of the well, he said, "This time I'm going to give you a violin, and you can play on the violin."

And the boy said, "I never could play anything in my life."

But the eagle said, "That's all right. I'm going to give you the power to play any kind of music you want. And I'm going to give you pencils and a brush and the ability to paint. You can paint for the king and be the best artist around."

When the youngest son was almost home, he went to stay with a poor man, not far from his father's palace. He still had a little money in his pocket, so he could pay him something.

The poor man was a shoemaker, and the youngest son offered to help him. The shoemaker was going to make some shoes for the princess with the golden hair, who was now planning to marry one of the older brothers.

The boy took an old piece of hide, and although he was not a shoemaker, through magic help he made a fine shoe —just one—and sent it to the princess by the shoemaker. When the old shoemaker took the shoe into the palace the duck started to quack and sing, the horse started to jump and neigh, and the girl laughed. The old king asked why everyone was so happy.

The girl put on the shoe, and it fit exactly. She liked it so well that she told the shoemaker she wanted another shoe made to match that one, and she wanted the one who made it to bring it in.

So the next day the youngest son came in, bringing the second shoe; when he got there, the duck sang and quacked continually, and the horse reared and plunged and neighed, and the girl laughed almost all the time.

The old king said, "There's something strange about all this."

Then the youngest son said to him, "What do you think should be done to a man who would kill his own brother, for no reason at all, and take all his possessions, and pretend that they were his?"

The king said, "I don't know what I would do—or what should be done."

The oldest brother said, "I know what I would do. I'd hitch four pair of horses to such a man—one pair to each hand and foot, and drive them off in different directions, so that they'd tear him to pieces."

The second brother said, "I'd take a block of wood and hang him upside down, with a razor attached, so that he would be cut to pieces and die a hard death."

Then the youngest brother said, "That's what my brothers did to me."

He told his father, "I'm your youngest son, and this is my bird, my horse, and my girl. My brothers tried to kill me and thought they had—then they took them all away from me."

The king had two pair of oxen brought in and hitched to the first brother, so that he was killed the way he had suggested, and the second brother, as he had said, with the razor and block of wood.

The youngest son married the girl.

# 46. The Boy Who Wouldn't Tell His Dream

A BOY, ten or twelve years old, had always taken the sheep to the hills, but one day he wouldn't get up. His mother urged him to get dressed and do his work, but he wouldn't do it. She told his father and he tried—but the boy stayed in bed, because he wanted to finish his dream.

When he did get up, he told his mother he'd had a dream, but when she didn't say anything—she was supposed to wish him good luck for his dream—he wouldn't tell his dream to her, nor to his father, since neither wished him good luck. So the father got a stick and drove him away.

The boy went to live at the home of a rich man, who had a daughter about his own age, so the boy and girl played together and had a good time.

One day the girl said, "Don't you have a father and mother?"

The boy said that he did, but that they had driven him away from home when he wouldn't tell his dream. The girl told her father, and the father asked the boy to tell his dream, but since he didn't wish him good luck, he wouldn't do it.

As the father had fed, clothed, and housed the boy for

some time now, he was very angry about this and had the boy put down in a dry pit a hundred feet deep. The guard didn't want to kill the boy, so he threw food down to him —bread, chicken, meat, and so on. Finally the guard managed to get a spade and throw it down to the boy, who decided to try to dig himself out.

He kept digging and digging and finally saw daylight, but thought he had better wait until dark to get out. When he came out, he found that he was in the same place—in the rich man's yard. He climbed the high fence, went into the house, and, looking around, saw the girl sleeping. He stepped into the room and kissed her.

At first the girl was angry and threatened to kill him, but finally asked him where he had come from. He told her she couldn't kill him—that probably nobody could.

The boy was dirty from digging himself out of the hole, and needed a shave and many other things. So the girl hid him, had the guard bring clothes for him, give him a bath, and so on. Nobody but the girl knew the boy was there.

One day the girl went to her father and mother and came back to the boy crying. A rich king had threatened to make war upon her father, unless he could tell which was the bottom and top of a stick. The boy had the stick sent in, so that he could try it out in water and mark it. He knew the bottom, the heavier part, would sink. The girl took the stick back to her parents the next morning, pretending she had discovered the bottom. The agreement was that nobody was to step outside that morning.

The rich king agreed that he couldn't fight on that question, but he sent the father another task. This time he sent a roll of two hundred pounds of salt through which the father was to make a hole. The boy accomplished the task the next morning, under the same conditions—nobody was to step outside—by putting a knife through the salt and leaving it there. Again the girl told her father she had done this, and again the rich king had no excuse to fight her father.

Then the girl went to her father and confessed that, not she, but the boy he had put in the 100-foot hole had done all this, and told him that he knew a lot of other tricks. The father sent for the boy, after promising not to harm him, and offered his daughter to him in marriage. However, the boy refused, because the father had not yet said the right thing. When the father wished him good luck for his dream, the boy agreed to marry the daughter, but said he would marry first the white girl—the man's daughter—and then a black girl—the rich king's daughter. The father agreed to this, offering to send thousands of soldiers along to help, but the boy said he wanted to go by himself, which he did.

First he put his ear to the ground, saying he was listening to the grinding of hundreds of pounds of salt being thrown away. A man passing by was frightened by all this and offered to follow the boy, since he had said he was on his way to the palace of the rich king. By other seemingly impossible tricks, such as drinking a river dry—he put his mouth to the water and said, "River, be dry, dry, dry," after which it all disappeared—he got four or five additional followers.

When he came to the palace of the rich king, he said he had come to marry the ruler's daughter, the princess. Everyone was surprised, since he had no army and few followers, and some tasks were set for him to do. First, they killed many camels and brought many pounds of salt, all of which he was to eat. He did, or *seemed* to do it, possibly by magic powers, and said, "Bring some more! Bring some more!"

By his powers of trickery and magic, by his intelligence and quick thinking, he outwitted them all, performing every task set for him or coming out first in each contest. In a handicap race, in which he had to carry an old woman on his shoulders, he won by the use of three tricks or unusual powers—by taking twenty-mile steps, by getting one of his opponents drunk so that he slept several hours while the others went on, and by stepping on another man's shoulder and pushing him down in the ground so that he could not move until someone rescued him. Finally, he surrounded the city with water, and the rich king gave up and told him to take the girl and go.

The boy did, all by himself. Each of his followers remained where he had found him, and he and the daughter of the rich king went back alone. There he married, first the white girl—the rich man's daughter—and then the black girl—the daughter of the rich king who had threatened to make war on the country.

# IX

## Spirits of the Dead

## 47. The Invited Guest

MANY YEARS AGO, two young friends had a very unusual experience. When the two were old enough to seek their fortunes, it became necessary for them to go their separate ways. Before they separated they promised each other that if either should marry, he would invite the other to his wedding. Sometime later, one of the young men, Francis, died, and the other, Marion, was to be married.

On his wedding day Marion kept his promise and went to the grave of his friend to invite him to his wedding. Soon after he had made the invitation, Francis was stand-

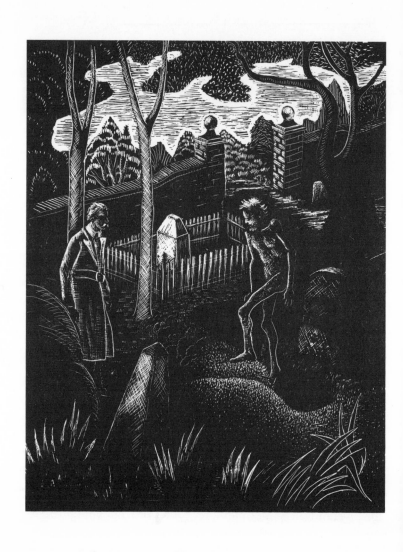

ing beside him. The two then left for the wedding. After the wedding ceremony, Francis asked Marion to come with him to his wedding, for he too was to be married on that day.

The two went directly from one wedding to the other, but the latter took place in a beautiful hall. There was magnificent music in the background which overwhelmed those present. After the musician had played one piece, Francis told Marion that it was time for him to leave, but Marion insisted on another piece and then another. After the conclusion of the third piece he was persuaded to leave.

When he arrived home he noticed that a great change had taken place in his hometown during his absence. He could not understand the change, for it seemed he had been gone only a short while.

He saw a young man along the road and began questioning him. The man did not know who Marion was nor did he know any of the people about whom he was asked. Marion learned that a story of a man who had left his wedding and had never returned was well known among the residents of the little European town. When he asked the location of the house of this man, he was shown a group of trees and told that the house no longer stood there, for the incident had taken place 300 years earlier.

Marion could not believe his ears, yet it was true. His presence in the beautiful hall had had a strange effect upon him. Every time the musician had played for what seemed only a few minutes, one hundred years had passed. It seemed incredible that the magnificence and splendor of the unknown place had had the power to make one hundred years seem like a few minutes, but Marion knew that it had happened.

# 48. The Fate of Frank McKenna

AT THE HIP of one of the mountainous hills that divide the county of Tyrone lived a man named McKenna. This McKenna had two sons, one of whom was in the habit of tracing hares on Sundays whenever there was a fresh fall of snow. His father, it seems, had frequently remonstrated with him about what he considered to be a violation of the Lord's day, as well as for his general neglect of mass. The young man, however, though otherwise harmless and inoffensive, was in this matter quite insensible to paternal reproof and continued to trace whenever labor would allow it.

One Christmas morning there was a deep fall of snow, and young McKenna got down his cockstick—a staff much thicker and heavier at one end than at the other—and prepared to set out on his favorite amusement. His father, seeing this, reproved him seriously and insisted that he attend prayers. His enthusiasm for the sport, however, was far stronger than his love of religion, and he refused to be guided by his father's advice. During the argument, the old man got warm and, finding that the son obstinately scorned his authority, knelt down and prayed that if the boy persisted in following his own will, he might never return from his hunting, unless as a corpse.

The imprecation, which was certainly as harsh as it was impious and senseless, might have startled many a mind. It had no effect, however, upon the son, who is said to have replied that, whether he ever returned or not, he was determined on going, and go, accordingly, he did. He was not alone, however, for it appears that three or four of the neighboring young men accompanied him.

Toward the latter part of the day, the young men followed a larger and darker hare than any of them had ever seen; she kept dodging them bit by bit, leading them to suppose that every succeeding cast of the cockstick would bring her down. It was observed afterward that she also led them into the recesses of the mountains, and that, although they tried to turn her course homeward, they could not succeed in doing so.

As evening advanced, the companions of McKenna began to feel the folly of pursuing her farther and to perceive the danger of losing their way in the mountains, should night or a snowstorm come upon them. They therefore proposed to give over the chase and return home, but McKenna would not hear of it. "If you wish to go home, you may," said he. "As for me, I'll never leave the hills till I have her with me."

They begged and entreated him to desist and return, but all to no purpose. At length, on finding him invincibly obstinate, they left him pursuing the hare directly into the heart of the mountains, and returned to their respective homes.

In the meantime one of the worst snowstorms ever remembered in that part of the country came on, and the self-willed young man was given up as lost. As soon as the storm was over, the neighbors assembled in a body and proceeded to look for him. The snow, however, had fallen so heavily that not a single footmark could be seen. Nothing but one wide waste of white hills met the eye, wherever they turned. No trace of McKenna was found.

His father, now remembering what he had said, was nearly distracted; for, although the body had not been found, escape or survival was felt to be impossible. They searched and searched but to no avail.

At length there came a thaw, and the youth's body was found on a snowdrift, lying in a surprising posture within a circle, which he had drawn around him with his cockstick. His prayer book lay opened upon his mouth, and his hat was pulled down, so as to cover it and his face. It is unnecessary to say that his death and the circumstances surrounding it created a most extraordinary sensation in the community.

Now, it so happened that the house nearest the spot where he lay was inhabited by a man named Daly, who was a caretaker. The situation of this house was the most lonely and desolate-looking that could be imagined. All this left a deep impression on the minds of the people.

An incident is said to have occurred at the funeral in keeping with the wild spirit of the whole melancholy event. During the procession a large dark-colored hare, which was instantly recognized by those who had been out with McKenna on the hills as the identical one that led him to his fate, is said to have crossed the road about twenty yards or so before the coffin. The story goes that a man struck it on the side with a blow that would have killed any ordinary hare. However, the blow not only did it no injury, but occasioned a sound to proceed from the body resembling the hollow one emitted by an empty barrel when struck.

In the meantime, the sensation began to die away in the natural progress of time. Then suddenly a report ran abroad like wildfire that, to use the language of the people, "Frank McKenna was appearing!"

One night, about two days after the funeral, the daughter of Daly, while lying in bed saw what appeared to be the likeness of McKenna. She screamed out, and, covering her head with the bedclothes, told her father and mother that Frank McKenna was in the house. Although the house was searched, nothing could be found of him.

Accordingly the girl soon fell asleep, and her father attributed what she had seen to fear or some accidental combination of shadows proceeding from the furniture. But the fears of the daughter began to return. Every night at the same hour, McKenna would reappear.

Finally the girl began to become so familiarized with the apparition that she overcame her terror sufficiently to venture to address it. She asked why he chose to appear to her instead of his own family. The ghost answered that he was not allowed to speak with any of his friends, for he had parted with them in anger. He said that they were quarreling about his breeches—a new pair that he had had made for Christmas Day, but he thought the old ones would do better, and didn't put the new pair on. He said his reason for appearing was for her to tell his friends that none of them were to wear them. The pants must be given to charity. These words were communicated to the family.

The conversations between the ghost and the girl now became not only frequent but also quite friendly and familiar. The Daly's place became a favorite haunt of his. The whole neighborhood was now in a state of commotion with this story of the apparition, and persons incited by curiosity began to visit the girl, in order to satisfy themselves of the truth of what they had heard.

The spot where the body of McKenna was found is now marked by a little heap of stones, which has been collected since the melancholy event of his death. Every person who passes it throws a stone upon the heap. But why this is practiced, or what it means, is not known, unless it is simply to mark the spot as a visible means of preserving the memory of the occurrence.

## 49. The Corpse That Wouldn't Stay Buried

IT WAS the custom in Czechoslovakia for young men to go into the army at the age of twenty-one and serve for six years. A young man named Philip had served but three years when he was killed. His body was returned home and properly buried in the cemetery.

The next day the caretaker found the grave open and the open coffin beside it, as if it had never been buried. This was very strange, and many people wondered about it. The priest and the caretaker reburied the soldier, but the next day the same thing happened. After the third time, the caretaker put the coffin in the cottage where he kept his tools and equipment.

Time went on, and people no longer talked of the soldier who would not stay buried. The caretaker had a hen, and she went every day to the cottage, flew up to the coffin, and laid an egg beside the feet of the soldier. When the caretaker wanted to take the eggs, a voice spoke up, "Leave them alone. They are not to be taken yet."

This frightened him, and he left them alone. He even made jokes about this soldier who would not remain buried and yet kept eggs for himself, even though he could not eat them.

There lived in the village a very pretty and popular girl. Young Philip and she had been very much in love. After he had gone into the army, she was courted by many suitors. She was very sad when she learned of his death, but in time let herself be persuaded by her mother and father to marry someone else. As was the custom, everyone in the village was invited to the wedding feast to partake of the music, dancing, drink, and food. At such times there was always much gaiety and also much foolishness—but all in good fun, for everyone was happy at a wedding.

When the bride and groom returned from church, many of the older guests were already warm with wine. Almost everyone was full of jests, and one man got up and challenged anyone to go to the caretaker's cottage and get the eggs from the dead soldier. One man, who had had more wine than the others and was already unsteady on his feet, accepted the challenge. All the guests clapped their hands and urged him on. A wager of drinks was set up, and he left.

At the caretaker's cottage he started to put the eggs into his hat when a voice spoke up, as if from the soldier, although he did not see the lips move. "Since you take the eggs to the wedding, you will have to take me too."

Thinking this a jest, the man answered boldly, "Why not? There is always room for more at a feast. Put your arms around my neck and I'll carry you." And he did.

When the drunken guest reached the bride's home, he left the soldier outside, propped up against the wall by the door, where he stood, stiff and tall, his eyes closed as if he were a sentry asleep at his post. Only one arm moved out a little.

The drunken guest took the hat full of eggs to his fellow conspirators, won the bet of extra drinks and applause, and was quite content. But the soldier at the door put a hush on the festivity, and some of the guests did not speak kindly of the man who had brought him there. He told them that the soldier had asked him to bring him, so he could do nothing else.

Everyone knew that there must be some reason that the soldier would not remain buried—that his soul was not at peace—and speculated about what unfinished deed was troubling him so that he could not rest.

Finally the priest, who was also at the wedding, asked that everyone pray for the release of the poor soldier's soul so that he could go back to the grave where he belonged. But after the amen, the soldier still stood there, stiff and straight, and would swing out his arm as if wanting to shake hands. The priest said perhaps the soldier wanted to bid farewell to all his good neighbors and friends, so everyone lined up and went by and shook hands with the soldier.

The bride was last. She was very pale. She knew why he was there, but still had not said anything. When she put her hand into the soldier's, he clasped it tight and would not let it go.

Finally, with great weeping, she confessed that she and Philip had made a vow to marry only each other, and she had broken the vow by marrying someone else. Still the soldier would not let go of her hand.

The priest thought a moment and said, "Very well, you made your vow. You can still keep it. I shall say the marriage vows over you here and now."

And thus it was. When the final amen was said, the soldier let go of the bride's hand and vanished—in the twinkling of an eye—as if he had never been there. When the guests went to the caretaker's cottage, they found that the coffin and body were gone. The open grave was filled up and even a fine sod covered it. The soldier's soul was at rest.

# 50. A Visit from the Dead

IN THE LATTER part of the nineteenth century, in the small town of Frascati, which was located on the outskirts of Rome, lived my maternal Great-Aunt Mary and her family. Aunt Mary, I have been told, was an unusually kindhearted person and a devoted mother. On sunny days she could often be seen in the vineyards with her husband and three little daughters, laughing and working, in a kind of ideal family setting. All this was before the plague struck the small town of Frascati.

Before the next three months had passed, my great-aunt suddenly became a victim of this killing fever and within a short time died. Two years after her death, my Great-Uncle Joseph, who was still sick with grief, remarried mainly for the sake of his three motherless little girls. Although his new wife was healthy and hard-working, she seemed to lack Aunt Mary's kindness, which was quickly sensed by the children.

After Uncle Joseph left to tend his vineyards each morning, the stepmother dressed up, locked the food in a smokeroom, and went to town for the day. She left the little girls all by themselves from late morning to early evening with neither food nor water. They dared not tell my uncle because their stepmother would only have punished them more cruelly.

One evening, upon her return from town, the stepmother found that some food had been taken from the smokehouse. Also, she noticed that her little stepdaughters had been cleaned up and well-fed. She knew that they had not taken the food themselves, because the youngest girl was only two years old and the oldest, although she was five, was crippled. When she asked the little girls how they had managed to reach the food, they told her that their mother had come and prepared their meal. After the stepmother had heard their story, she punished them harshly and vowed to hide the food more securely.

The next morning, she hid the supplies in a secret place before she left, but upon her return, again found that food had been prepared for the children. Now she knew that surely someone must have been feeding her stepdaughters each day, and she decided to see who it was.

The next morning instead of going to town, the stepmother hid in the old barn behind the house. She waited and waited, but she saw no one enter the home. Suddenly she heard laughter coming from within the walls. She quickly ran to the door and stood, listening to the conversation inside the room. Were her ears playing tricks on her? She knew that the voice she heard must have been a product of her imagination, because the voice sounded like the girls' mother—but she was dead! Caught by curiosity and emotion, she pushed the door open and entered the room.

There before her stood the little girls' mother. Aunt

Mary, I have been told, warned her never to treat the girls cruelly again. The stepmother, seized by fear, turned to run, and as she did, this ghostly figure grabbed her arm, leaving a branded "M" in remembrance of the warning.

That very evening the stepmother packed her clothes and was never seen by my Uncle Joseph again. I have been told that she wandered from place to place in Italy the rest of her life, telling the story of her strange experience. Although many people have concluded that her feeling of guilt concerning the little girls might have made her imagine the vision of my great-aunt, no one in my family to this day has ever explained the branded "M" on her arm.

# $\overline{x}$

## Luck, Wealth, and Good Fortune

## 51. King Neptune's Diamonds

THERE ONCE WAS an old man who lived with his son in a deep forest. They lived in a log cabin, not far from a lake, which the man said was haunted. He warned his son not to go near it, as he might be killed. The boy wandered far and wide, but never went near the lake. He had a swimming hole where he could catch fish, so the lake was not too much temptation.

Wherever he went, he carried a heavy club—the only weapon he had. Several times a bear had attacked him, but he always beat it off with the club. The bears in the vicinity knew him and avoided him. He loved the young bear cubs and loved to play with them. He was twenty-four years old and stronger than any bear in the forest. Many times he walked without his club. The bears knew him and did not bother him. He was the king of the forest.

One nice morning he thought to himself, "Why shouldn't I go near the lake? What have I got to be afraid of? Father wouldn't need to know."

Taking his favorite club, he walked toward the forbidden spot. About twenty feet from the water's edge, he sat down on a rock and watched the lake. It was beautiful. The sun was about man-high in the sky and reflected beautifully in the water. "What a nice place to swim!" he thought.

He took his clothes off and started for the water. All at once something popped out of the lake. With a kind of grunt, it splashed from the water and walked toward him. The boy jumped back, got his club, and patiently waited for the ugly figure to charge. It was smaller than a bear and had a curious club, with three sharp points on the end, in its hands.

The boy stood as still as a statue, awaiting the attack. The monster edged, foot by foot, toward him. It had long whiskers that came almost to its knees and black, piercing eyes. Like a tiger it sprang at the youth striking with the forklike club. At the same time the boy brought down his club with such force that it struck his opponent's weapon from his hands and broke his own club in half. In surprise, the half-fish stopped in his tracks. For a moment, the two eyed each other. Then the half-man, half-fish jumped on the boy. They grappled and rolled, but the boy could not get hold of the cricketlike creature. It was wet and slimy like a fish.

In the meantime the sun was getting hotter, and the monster was getting drier. By noon he was dry and tired out. The boy grabbed him by the neck and held him down, helpless. The figure quivered under the boy's strength. "Please, let me go," he cried.

"Not so fast. Tell me who you are."

"I am King Neptune. I live in the lake. On the bottom is my castle. If you will let me go free, I will repay you a million times. All the treasure on the bottom of the sea is mine. I will bring you as many diamonds as you can carry."

"How do I know you are telling the truth and will come back at all? How do I know but what next time you will ambush me and kill me?"

"What!" cried the creature. "I am a king and a king never goes back on his word. And I promise that I will never hurt human beings again."

"I'll take your word." And the boy let King Neptune go free.

The king got up, shook hands with the boy, and said, "I'll be back in half an hour."

"Good," said the boy. "I'll wait for you."

The scaly man jumped into the lake to get the diamonds. The boy jumped into the lake also to wash the mud from his body. When he was clean, he put his clothes on again, and waited for the sea-king.

In a few minutes there was a disturbance on the lake, and the king appeared. He had a bag in his hands as big as a young bear cub.

"Here are the diamonds!" He gave the bag to the boy and jumped back into the lake. Nobody ever saw him again.

The boy was curious. He opened the bag, thrust his

hand in it, and brought out a handful of precious stones. He looked at them and, thinking they were candies, put one in his mouth.

"Bah!" He spit it out. "Shiny rocks! Such things are for babies to play with. I could choke that creature and feed his body to the fishes!"

He put the bag of diamonds on his shoulder and started toward home. When he came to the wood shanty, he threw the bag on the woodpile and went into the house.

"Where have you been all this time?" the old man asked.

"I was playing with some young bear cubs I found this morning."

"I was thinking that tomorrow I would take you to town —a place you've never been—and buy you anything you want. You are a good boy, and sooner or later you will have to see the world."

Early the next morning, they saddled their horses and rode out of the woods together. When they came to the end of the forest, the sun was high in the sky. Some distance ahead, there was a big stone house, where some rich man lived.

"Is that the town?" the boy asked.

"No, Son. That is only a house."

"It's pretty," the boy said.

He stopped his horse and looked at the pretty white house. At that moment, something very beautiful appeared at the door. It had on a white dress, and had pretty red cheeks.

"Hello," it said, with a smile.

The boy stared with amazement at the apparition. Then he spurred his horse and shot like an arrow to his father.

"Father, you said that you'd buy me anything I wanted."

"Yes, I will," the old man said. "What do you want?"

207

"I'll show you what I want." He galloped back to the door and pointed at the girl. "See, Father, buy me this."

The astonished girl ran into the house. She didn't know what this was all about. The old man was puzzled too.

"I don't know, Son. Nobody can buy that, probably, but I'll try. Let's go into town now. Maybe you'll like something better there."

When they got into town, the father showed him pretty gold watches, rings, all kinds of toys, musical instruments, and everything the old man could think of.

"No, Father. I don't want anything like that. If you don't want to buy me what we saw on the doorstep, I don't want anything else."

With a heavy heart, the old man rode out of town with his son. When they came to the white house, the boy got down from his horse.

"Come on, Father. Don't be like King Neptune. Keep your word."

"All right, Son. I'll see what I can do." The old man knocked at the door.

In a moment the door was opened by the girl, who asked "What can I do for you?"

"I'd like to see your father," the old man answered.

"He's in the hall. Would you come in? Father, someone wants to see you!"

The door opened and a well-dressed man appeared. He had a diamond-studded pin in his necktie, as big as a grain of corn, and a diamond ring on his finger.

"I'd like to talk to you in private," said the old woodsman.

"Of course. Come into the hall."

When the forester explained his visit, the rich man laughed. "Your son is a fine lad, but you're just a working-man, and my daughter is not used to work. You see, it couldn't be done."

When the old man came out of the hall, he looked ten years older.

"What's wrong, Father?" the boy asked.

"Well, if I had as many diamonds as he has, then I could buy what you want."

"The shiny stones? How many do you need?"

"Oh, a handful," the old man answered.

"That's easy," said the boy. "I'll bring a thousand of them. Wait here. I'll be back before dark."

The lad did not wait for an answer. He jumped on his horse and shot like lightning into the forest. For two long hours the old man waited and worried. He didn't know what to think of his son. At last he heard the drumming of hoofbeats. The boy dismounted and handed a bag to his father.

"Here, Father. Shiny stones—lots of them."

Together the two fathers examined the bag of diamonds.

The next day a big wedding was held. Everybody was happy, especially the old forester, because he was able to buy his son what he wanted most.

# 52. The Three Godfathers

ONE TIME three godfathers went out to look for a place where somebody had buried money. Two of the godfathers said, "Let's go dig for the treasure."

But the third godfather wouldn't go. The others coaxed him, but he still wouldn't go. He went on home and went to sleep.

The two others went and dug—dug until the middle of the night—and found a big snake. They decided to go home, then, so they killed the snake and took it with them.

Before they reached the third godfather's house, one of them said, "Let's throw that snake into his house."

There was a little door—where the cat could get in and out—so they threw the snake in through the door.

When the third godfather woke up, he saw a bright, shining light made by a golden snake.

In the morning he took the snake to the city to find out what it was worth. The jeweler said, "$60,000," so the godfather sold it and went home.

He asked his wife if the others had been there and she said they hadn't, so he told her not to tell them about it.

The second godfather was worried. The godfather who got the gold started to improve his house and seemed to have plenty of money. And he had never said a word about the snake they had dug up and thrown into his house.

Finally the second godfather asked him, "How did you get the money to do the things you do?"

The third godfather said, "Do you remember when you went out to dig for a treasure?"

The second godfather said he did.

"That night my room shone like gold when I woke up. And when I went where the light was, I found a golden snake."

The second godfather said, "I threw that snake in there. We found it when we went to dig for the treasure. We dug till the middle of the night and found only that snake. So we threw it in your place and went home."

And that's how luck was missed by the first two godfathers, but came to the third one.

# 53. Blind Wolf

THIS ALL HAPPENED a long time ago—I don't know how many hundred years ago—but one man was so poor he could hardly get along—always poor.

He had a woman, who said, "Well, man, what are you going to do? I'm poor and you're poor all the time. What are you going to do about it?"

"Well," the man said, "God did that. I can't help it. You know, poor is poor."

He went to the village, and at the village he was given some kind of stock—a calf or cow, a lamb or sheep—something. Every year somebody gave him some kind of seed, some kind of drink, and some kind of stock. And every day he would go out and take care of the sheep.

One day he took the sheep to the top of the hill. When he wanted to take them home, so the woman could get the milk, one sheep didn't want to go, but kept trying to go down to the creek bottom. He thought to himself, "Is that sheep crazy? Where is it going? I'm going to follow it."

He followed the sheep down to the bottom of the creek. There was a wolf down there, and the sheep lay down beside it, so that it could have some of her milk, and it did. The man looked at the wolf, and saw it was blind. Then he took his sheep and other stock home. He threw his stick away and lay down on the bed.

He said, "I saw a blind wolf. I'm not going to work any more."

He lay there on the bed, and after a while the woman came in and said, "Man, get up! All the rest have put their sheep and lambs and cattle outside."

He said, "No woman. I'm not going to do it. I saw a blind wolf."

The woman said, "You're not going to do it? Are you going to stay hungry?"

"Oh," he said, "I saw a blind wolf."

He wouldn't go, so the woman went herself. Down at the creek she saw a nice, smooth stone.

She thought to herself, "I like that stone!"

Lifting the stone she saw that underneath it was a container of gold—a big pot, full of gold; she was terribly excited.

She put the top back and wondered what to do. "I can't take it home," she thought. She took the stock to graze, and when she got home the man was still lying on the bed. She said, "Hey, man, get up! I've found a lot of gold. God gave it to me." She knew where the gold was, of course.

The man said, "Don't bother me, woman. I saw a blind wolf. Don't bother me, I say. Don't bother me."

She said, "What's the matter with you? There's lots of gold. Come on, now. Get up and go and bring it home."

He said, "No, I'm not going to do it. I saw a blind wolf."

The woman went to the neighbor's house next door, and said, "Neighbor, will you go with me and help me? My man won't go. There's gold—I've found a pot full of gold, but I can't bring it home. I'll show you where it is, if you'll take a sack and fill it and bring it home. Then you can have half and I'll take half."

The neighbor man agreed to this, and the two went for the gold, but the husband just lay there on the bed. He wouldn't get up.

They found the rock and the pot of gold, and the man filled the sack, put it on his shoulder and carried it home. When they were almost there, he said, "Woman, I'll take the gold over to my house—the whole sack. You go and tell your man to come, and we'll divide it up."

The woman said, "All right."

So the neighbor man took the gold home. He wanted to steal that gold and started to open the sack before the man got there. He thought that he would get all that he could.

He opened the sack—and the sack was full of snakes.

He said, "Tighten up! Tighten up!" The snakes were about to crawl all over the house and kill everybody. "Tighten up!" he said, and he pulled the drawstrings.

The woman had gone over to tell her husband. She

213

said, "Man, get up! Go over to the next house and divide up the gold."

He said, "Woman, don't bother me. I saw a blind wolf."

About that time the neighbor had picked up the sack, carried it over to his neighbor's and poured the whole thing into the window, cursing as he did so.

But, as he poured the contents of the sack out, it was all gold again.

The husband saw this and said, "I told you I saw a blind wolf!"

Now that he was rich, there was no need to do anything but have a good time.


## 54. The Fortuneteller


ONCE THERE were two brothers who lived with their father on a small farm in Italy. Everyone was happy until the father died. In his will he said that half of his farm would go to one son, and the other half to the other. The eldest son was named Bird and the youngest, Grasshopper.

Everything was going fine until Grasshopper noticed one day that his part of the wheat was dying. He didn't know what was causing this, so one night he told his brother that he was going out into the field to see what was happening to his half of the farm. Each man had a woman who was supposed to take the weeds out of the wheat each night. The woman that Bird had was a good worker, but when she pulled the weeds from the wheat she would put them on Grasshopper's land.

Since Grasshopper had a lazy woman, she did not clean out the wheat, but would go to sleep under a big tree every night. When the young man saw this he was angry and told her to leave. The woman, not having anywhere to go, had to think of something fast. She told him that she did not clean out the wheat because he was not meant to be a farmer, but a fortuneteller. Grasshopper told her that he knew nothing about fortunetelling, but if that was what he was supposed to do, he would try.

The next day Grasshopper got ready to go to the town to become a fortuneteller. On his way, he saw the king out fox hunting. The king, seeing him, asked where he was going. Grasshopper put his head down and told the king that he was going to the town to become a fortuneteller. While the young man had his head down, the king caught a grasshopper on a tree limb and held it in his hand. The king said, "So you want to become a fortune-teller. Well, if you can tell my fortune, I will believe you."

When the king said this, Grasshopper didn't know what to do. He put his head down and started to pray, but it was mostly muttering. He was saying to himself, "Poor Grasshopper, what are you going to do now?"

When the king heard this, he thought he was talking to the insect he held. Since he knew that Grasshopper didn't know what he had in his hand, he said, "You must have some special power. Come to the palace with me."

When they got to the palace, the king told the youth that the queen was going to have a baby; and asked if he could tell whether it would be a boy or a girl. Grasshopper didn't know what to do, for he knew nothing about fortunetelling. Finally, after worrying all day, he thought, "If I tell the king that I will have to see the queen without any clothes on, she will say, 'No,' and that will end it."

The queen did say "No," but the king decided she must do as the youth said. When Grasshopper looked at her from the front, he said, "Well, it looks like a girl." But when he looked at her from the back, he said, "Still, it looks like a boy."

It just so happened that the queen had twins, one boy and one girl. Grasshopper lived happily with the king and the queen for the rest of his life.

# 55. The Dream

ABOUT FIVE O'CLOCK in the morning Mrs. Lopez was telling her husband about a dream that she had had that night. She dreamed that someone told her to dig behind the little country church in their town, and there she would find great quantities of money. However, her husband did not think that this was possible.

Two men, who came for Mr. Lopez to go to work in the morning, stood behind the door listening to what his wife said. They decided to investigate and immediately turned back and went to this church. There they dug for some time and found many snail shells, but didn't find the money Mrs. Lopez had talked about. They thought therefore, that she was just playing a joke on them.

The two men took the several bushels of shells they had found and went to the home of Mr. and Mrs. Lopez while they were sleeping. They climbed to the roof and made a hole big enough to throw the shells down. The shells fell on the bed where Mr. and Mrs. Lopez lay, and when they landed, they all turned into money. Mr. Lopez didn't know what happened. He couldn't understand it at all, but Mrs. Lopez said, "See, this is the money I was telling you about."

# XI

## Religious Stories

## 56. Christ and the Blacksmith

ONE TIME there was a blacksmith who wanted to be called master above all the other masters. He wanted to be called "Headmaster," and was insulted if anybody said "Master."

This was during the time that Christ was traveling the world. So one day Christ came along and said, "Good morning, Master."

And the blacksmith said, "Who are you? Get out of here!"

"What is your title?" Christ asked.

"Headmaster," the blacksmith said.

"Do you think you deserve that title?"

"Yes," said the blacksmith. "I can do more than anyone at my trade."

Christ intimated that he might be able to do more.

The blacksmith said, "You'll have to prove it."

Christ took up an old man, put him in the fire until his flesh was burned off, then put him on the anvil and started to beat him with a cane. Then, flash—a young man came out.

"Can you do that?" Christ said.

The blacksmith said, "I've got my dad. I'll make a young man out of him. If you can do it, I can do it better."

He dragged the old man down, put him on the fire to burn, and waited. When only a few bones were left, he put him on the anvil and started to beat him with the cane—but nothing happened.

# 57. The Boy Who Made a Trip to Hell

THERE ONCE lived a poor peasant with his wife, on a small farm. He was so poor he did not even have an ox to plow with, but dug all his ground with a mattock.

One day while he swung the mattock on the hard ground, a well-dressed stranger came along. He had a gold watch and heavy chain that shone like the sun.

"Why don't you plow?" he asked. "Digging all this ground with a mattock is too hard on your back."

The poor man stood speechless, gazing openmouthed at

the intruder's spotless clothes. "What else can I do? I have no ox, and no money to buy one."

"Oh," said the stranger, "there's lots of money. What you have to do is sell something."

"I have nothing to sell."

"Yes you have. I'll give you all the money you can carry for the thing that you don't know you have."

The poor man was puzzled. What could it be that he would not know about? Everything he had ran through his mind. "All right, Mister. There isn't a thing I wouldn't know. You can have whatever you want, if you'll give me the money."

"Wait a minute," said the rich man. "You sign this paper and the sack that is behind me is yours."

He stepped aside and the poor man saw a burlap sack, full of bills. Surprised beyond words, he thought, "What a life I would have if I owned that sack." Then he said aloud, "I'd be only too glad to sign, but I can't write."

"That's all right; just put 'X' on it, like this one. But don't make it like a cross. I don't like crosses."

"All right. I'll make ten X's for that sack, if you want me to."

"Oh, no. One will be enough."

When he made the sign, the stranger handed over the sack of money and said, "After seven years I'll come back and get the thing that you don't know you have."

"All right. You're welcome to it."

The poor peasant put the sack on his shoulder and started toward the house, as happy as he had ever been. "Rebecca! O Rebecca!"

Where could she be? She always waited for him on the bench outside the house. Probably she was busy setting the table for supper. He could hardly wait to see her face when he showed her the money. Like a young goat he rushed through the door.

"Look what I've got, Rebecca! All this sack full of bills is ours!" And he grabbed her with both hands. "Look, all ours!"

"Where did you get that?"

"Oh, some crazy man came and bought something of me that I didn't know I had, and after seven years he will come and get it. And for that, the fool gave me all this money!" Then he heard a muffled cry. "What's that?"

"That is your son you didn't know you had," the wife said. "And that was the devil that bought him from you. What are we going to do now?"

The years passed and the little baby grew into a husky boy and started to school. Every time his mother gave him his lunch for school, she cried.

One day he said, "Mamma, why do you cry every time you give me the lunch for school? If it is so hard on you, I can go without lunch."

"Oh, no. It is not the lunch." And then she told him all that had happened.

"Well, Mamma," he said, "don't cry. Something might happen to make everything all right."

By this time he was six and a half years old. On the way to school he passed a little chapel, in which was the statue of the Madonna and the little baby Jesus. The statue of Jesus held in one hand a little ball that represented the world. Every day he passed the chapel, he knelt down and prayed.

One day before his seventh birthday, he prayed as usual, and to his surprise, the Madonna stepped down from the altar, took the ball from the little Jesus' hand, and gave it to him.

222

"Throw this ball on the ground," she said. "The ball will roll, and you must follow; when you come to hell, demand the agreement that your father signed. You will be free when you get the paper. In case the devil will not give it to you, show him this ball and tell him that you will destroy his hell and all the devils if he doesn't. Don't be afraid of him. Go, and good luck!"

The boy gladly took the ball and threw it as he had been told. When it hit the ground, all the world was shaken. The ball rolled and the boy followed—across mountains and canyons and deserts. In a great hollow, in the middle of a dark woods, he met a man dressed in armor from head to toe.

"Hello, little boy," he said. "Where are you going?"

"I am going to hell after my father's agreement." And he told him all about it.

"Will you ask him if he's got my name? My name is Nick."

The boy said that he would, and told him to wait there for him.

Then the ball started rolling and the boy followed. When they came to an iron door, the ball bumped against it with a force that shook all hell, burst the heavy door off the hinges, and frightened the devils out of their wits. The big boss jumped out with only one horn on his head. The other one had been knocked off when the ball struck the door. He saw the boy with the ball—which he had picked up after it had struck the hell door, as instructed by the Madonna—in his hand.

"What are you doing with that ball? Get away from here! We don't like that ball," he yelled.

"I am not going away before I get the agreement my father signed nearly seven years ago," the boy said.

"Oh, yes," said the devil. "I know now who you are. I was the one who bought you, and tomorrow I will come and get you."

"Oh, no you won't. If you don't give me the agreement, I'll throw this ball at your hell and destroy it completely, together with all your devils."

"No, no, no!" cried the one-horned devil. "I'll give you the agreement back. Just hold the ball, please! I'll be back in a minute."

He ran back to his desk, grabbed the agreement, and came back in almost no time. "Here is your agreement. Now, please go. I will never bother you."

"Wait a minute," said the boy. "That's not all I want. I met Nick on the way. You know, the man in armor, who lives in the dark woods. He wants to know if you have his name here."

"Wait. I'll have to look at the scroll."

He brought out the lengthy list and looked to see if he had any Nick. "Yes, here it is. He is mine for sure. He killed ninety-nine men. How could *he* be saved?"

"You know," said the boy.

"Of course I know. Tell him to take a dead limb of an apple tree, go to the graveyard at midnight, stick the limb in the ground, and kneel and pray until the limb sprouts and starts to grow. Ha, ha, ha, ha!" And the devil laughed loudly.

The boy turned around and started back home. When he came to the dark woods, he met old Nick and told him what the devil had said.

"All right, my boy," Nick said. "Thank you very much. I'll try that."

He found a dead, dry limb of an apple tree, and at midnight went to the graveyard, stuck the limb in the soft earth, knelt down, and started to pray. Time passed. The clock struck one. Then he saw something moving. He listened. Somebody was digging. "It's a ghost," he thought to himself. "Let it dig."

Nick kept on praying. The ghost got angry at something and started swearing. Nick stopped praying and listened a little more carefully.

"That's no ghost," he thought. "Ghosts don't swear. It's a grave-robber, stealing a corpse. Well, I've killed ninety-nine men already. This will make one hundred even!"

Nick aimed and fired, and to his surprise, the dead limb immediately turned green, bloomed, and bore three apples. For the good deed that Nick had done in killing the grave-robber, God had forgiven him for the previous ninety-nine killings.

If you go in a Catholic church where they have a St. Nick, you will see he has three apples on his book. These are the apples that he picked at the graveyard, the night he killed the grave-robber.

# 58. He Walked on Earth

ONE MORNING a long time ago in a small village, an old man came walking into town. He had on shabby clothes, and wore a long beard. His cane was crooked, and his slippers were full of holes.

As he came to the center of the village, he saw a stream. He went to the stream, sat down, and put his feet into the water; he didn't even bother to take off his slippers.

He sat there for a while and a little girl came up to him. "Hello," she said, and he answered with a "Hello." Then he asked the little girl to wash his tired feet.

"No, I will not wash your dirty old feet," she answered.

"Why?" the old man asked.

The little girl ran away as fast as she could. Apparently she was afraid of him.

About ten minutes later another little girl came up to the old man. "Hello, sir," she said.

"Hello, little girl," the old man answered with a smile one could hardly see, because of his long beard.

He asked the little girl if she would wash his feet.

She said, "Yes, sir, I'll wash your feet."

So the little girl started. She took off the old man's slippers and washed his feet very gently, taking care not to hurt his tired feet. When the old man offered her a dime, she said she didn't want the money, and walked away. Then the old man disappeared and wasn't seen any more.

A few days later the little girl who wouldn't wash the old man's feet died. No one knows how or why.

Some people say that the old man was Jesus. The old folks say that Jesus walked the earth a long time ago as a beggar.

# 59. The Beggar's Bread

THERE WAS once a poor man who went about asking for something to eat. One woman became tired of him coming around begging for food, money, and clothes all the time and although she never gave him anything she decided to put an end to it. The next time she baked bread she made one nice small loaf, and within this loaf she put some poison.

Soon after this the poor man came to her house again begging for some food. He was surprised to receive a loaf of bread from the woman, and very happy about it. He took the bread home and, because it was such a nice loaf of bread, he decided to save it and eat his old bread first.

That night there was a severe storm and a soldier stopped at his home for shelter. The poor man didn't have anything to give his guest except the bread that the woman had given him, so he offered him that.

The soldier said, "That's all right. I don't want anything to eat. I just need some shelter from the rain," but the poor man insisted that he have some bread.

The soldier ate the bread and soon became deathly sick.

227

The house was too far from town to call a doctor, so the soldier died. The poor man journeyed to town to report the death, and a policeman and doctor came to investigate the cause. The doctor told them that the soldier had died from poisoning.

He asked the poor man where he got the bread that the soldier ate.

The poor man told him that a woman gave it to him and took the policeman and doctor to her house. When the policeman asked the poor man why he did not eat any of the bread, he said he had some old bread he wanted to finish first.

The policeman then took the woman along, and they all went back to the poor man's house, where the body was. Here the woman discovered that the soldier was her son, who was coming home on leave.

The poor man said to the woman, "You never did give anything to me except the nice loaf of bread, and I thought I was giving my best to the soldier. You didn't know that you were fixing it for your son. That's the way it happens for those who try to do the wrong thing. They do it to themselves."

# 60. The King's Unhappy Son

ONCE THERE was a king who had no male children. Every night he prayed for a son, and finally one was born to him, but when the boy became of age, he didn't want to see or talk to anyone. When the father invited young people in, the youth refused to have anything to do with them. The king didn't know what to do, so he called all the doctors in the land to his palace. He told them that his son would not talk to anyone or even look at them.

The doctors met for one week and finally they told the king that there was only one way to make the boy happy. The king was to find the happiest man in the land and get his shirt from him. Then he was to put the shirt on his son and this would make him happy. The king sent all his men over the land to look for the happiest man and to get his shirt.

Men were sent here, there, and everywhere. There were two men who had to go around a mountain to get to the town, but instead of going around the mountain, they decided to go over it. As soon as they got to the bottom, they saw a pasture with a man taking care of some sheep. When they got to the man, they asked him if he were happy. The man took his flute out and started to play. He said he had everything that he wanted. No one said anything to him there. He did as he pleased and had plenty of food, water, and fresh air. Then the men asked him again if he were happy and he said that he was the happiest man in the world.

"This is just the man that we are looking for," the men

said. They were happy not only for the king but also for the reward that they would get for finding the man.

The men stayed with the man for a week to make sure that he was really the happiest man in the world. When they asked him if he would do something for the king, he said he'd do anything for him. The men asked for his shirt, but he didn't know what they were talking about. They kept trying to explain, and finally got him to take off his sheepskin jacket, only to find that he was wearing nothing under it—no shirt.

No one in the rest of the land was as happy as this man, but since he had no shirt, the king's son still didn't talk or look at anyone.

# XII

# Family Relations

## *61.* The Snow Boy

ALEX ROSE had served in the armed forces during the war. At the conclusion of his service he returned home for the first time in nine years. He was very happy to see his wife, but was astonished to find a two-year-old boy in his home. His wife claimed that the boy was their son. Alex argued that it was impossible for him to have a son who was only two years old when he had not been home for nine years. His wife then proceeded to tell him the following story, which seemed to him too incredible to believe.

She said that on a particular day, she had been out of doors when, much to her amazement, snow began to fall from a sunny and cloudless sky, resting only on her chest. No snow had fallen on the ground beside her or elsewhere in her surroundings. It was a strange happening, and to climax the incident, she had given birth to a baby boy the following day, all of which she believed was due to the snow that fell upon her chest.

Alex did not believe the story his wife related, but decided to act as though he did. One day he took the boy for a walk and left him with a farmer and his family. When he returned home, instead of telling his wife what had actually happened, he told her that while he and the boy were walking, the child began to melt in the hot sun. The wife, knowing of the strange thing that had happened to her, believed the story.

The boy, then living at the farmhouse, proceeded along the path of strange happenings that had been characteristic of his life in the world up to that time. In the next two years he advanced in growth from two years to about twenty-one years.

All this was strange indeed, but to add to the strangeness of the happenings that had taken place during this segment of Alex's life was that two years after he had taken the boy away, there came a succession of snowfalls each night. The unusual part of all this was that the snow fell only on the house of Alex Rose.

Alex, remembering what his wife had told him about the birth of the boy, associated the series of snowfalls with the boy, and went to the farmer's house to find him. He realized that he had made a terrible mistake in taking the boy away, for he now believed that what his wife had told him was true. When he reached the farm, he found that the farmer, his family, and the boy had been

burned to death in the flames that had destroyed the
farmhouse on the night that the snowfalls had begun.

# 62. The Spendthrift Son

ONCE THERE was a wealthy man who had a son. The son
was always going out and spending money; his father
urged him to stop since someday he would run out of
money and lose all his friends. But the son would not
listen—and kept on spending his money.

As a result, the father prepared one of his rooms, taking
a section from the ceiling. He made a cardboard rafter
that was hollow inside and stuffed it with money. He
then tied a rope around it and replaced it so that it looked
as if it were part of the rafters.

When the son asked for more money, his father took
him to the room and showed him the rafter with the rope,
saying, "When I die and you run out of money and lose
all your friends, put this rope around your neck and hang
yourself here, as no one will look after you."

After the father died, it turned out the way he said it
would. The son ran out of money and sold his good
clothes, shoes, jewelry, and all that he owned. His clothes
turned into rags, and he was starving, as his friends had
forsaken him. He remembered what his father had said,
went to the room, and put the rope around his neck. As

he jumped from a chair to hang himself, the cardboard rafter broke in two, and out fell all the money.

He then realized what a good father he had had. It's never too late to learn a lesson, and he said, "God bless my father wherever he is."

He took the money and dressed up nicely. His so-called friends noticed and began to hang around him again, so he invited all of them to his house for dinner.

He then went to the butcher shop and bought a lot of soupbones and a steak. At the dinner the steak was served to him and his servant, and the soupbones were served to his friends.

His friends complained, "What kind of a friend is he? He eats steak and serves his guests soup and bones."

He answered them, "You ate all my meat before, and now all that is left is soup and bones."

# *63*. The Rooster

ONCE THERE was a husband and wife who lived on a farm. Wherever they went, they had to travel by donkey. One day they went to town, both riding on the donkey's back. The baby donkey followed his mother to town and called out, "Mother, wait for me! You are always hurrying."

The mother replied, "You can run and catch up with me. I have a big load on my back, and I have to walk fast so I can reach home and put it down."

The master heard them and laughed. His wife asked him what he was laughing about.

He said, "Oh, nothing."

She said, "There must be something. I want to know."

He said, "I can't tell you."

She kept asking him and saying, "I want to know. I want to know."

He said, "If you want me to tell you, I will; but you'll have to call the priest for me first, so I can confess, because I am going to die."

"Why are you going to die?"

He said, "If I tell you what you want to know, I will die."

His secret was that he could understand what animals said, and no one else could. He was the only person who could understand animals, because he was without sin. This secret he was supposed to keep to himself.

She said, "That's all right."

So she went to get the priest. While she was on her way, the man sat on the porch steps, watching the chickens and rooster in the yard.

The hens were saying to the rooster, "You act a fool all the time. Don't you know that our master is going to die?"

The rooster said, "That's because he's not smart. See how many of you there are? I keep you all under my control. Behind the door is a big club, and when his wife comes, if he wanted to, he could teach her to respect him."

The master heard this and got up from the steps and hid behind the door. When his wife came, he hit her on the head, knocking her down.

Soon the priest came and asked, "Who has to confess?"

The master pointed to his wife, who was on the floor, and said, "There she is."

The priest said, "But she just came to call me."

The master replied, "I'm sorry, but she's the one who is sick."

So the rooster saved his master's life.

# 64. A Long Wait

SEVERAL MONTHS after a young man and woman had been married, it was necessary for them to separate, as the husband could find no work. The eager and adventurous young man set out for a larger city to seek employment with the promise that he would either return or send for his wife within a very short time.

After being in the city for a few days, he located a job with a widower. He was to work on the man's farm, just outside town during the day, and be somewhat of a companion in his spare time. Since he was given a comfortable room and adequate wages, he accepted the job and began enjoying his independence and the liveliness of the big city—something to which he was not accustomed. He remained there working hard and having a good time, never once mentioning to his employer that he had a young bride waiting for him to return, yet he always remained faithful to her.

Thirty years passed and he had not mentioned his wife nor had he attempted to get in contact with her. The farmer, who had grown old, noticed a sudden change in his farmhand and asked if he were troubled. Being unable to keep his misdoings to himself any longer, he poured out the story of his life. The old man was most sympathetic, but stressed the fact that much wrong had already been done and it was now his duty to rectify his behavior.

The man pondered for several weeks over what he must do and then decided that he must return home to his wife. He packed his belongings and began his journey. He had not gone far, however, when he became worried and uneasy about returning. Consequently, he turned around and went back to the farmer's house.

The old man asked him why he had come back, and the man told him that he needed advice before he could carry out his plan. The farmer, not wanting to interfere but knowing the man's need for reassurance, told him to be careful not to comment upon or criticize anything he might see or hear while on his journey, and he would return with a clear mind. He again attempted to depart, but felt that he must have more advice.

Again, he sought words of wisdom from the old farmer and was told that near his hometown, he would find a new road that was much nicer than the old road. He said, however, that even though it would be a rougher and longer route, he should take the old road and under no circumstances should he travel on the new one.

Again the younger man left, but he still felt that he must have more advice. This time the old farmer simply told him, "Don't shoot at first sight," and wished him well on his journey.

Having no other mode of transportation, he began his journey by foot. He walked for several hours and became weary and hungry. Coming across a small inn along the road, he asked if he might stay there to rest and to get a meal. While he was eating, the innkeeper went out to the well, but instead of bringing up water, he had his wife in the bucket. He brought her in and fed her a meal in a skull, and then lowered her back in the well.

The man was appalled, but remembering the old farmer's advice, he made no comment. He remained at the inn for the night and arose early to continue his trip. The innkeeper stopped him and asked him why he did not comment on the manner in which he was punishing his wife. He replied that it was the innkeeper's affair, and he was not concerned.

The innkeeper was amazed at his reply and took him out to his backyard, which was lined with many graves. He explained that all these people had stopped at his inn and had attempted to stop him from keeping his wife in the well, so he had killed them. Being pleased that the present traveler was not concerned, he gave him a jug of his finest wine and sent him on his way.

As he neared his hometown, the traveler was weary. Then a young man came by in a carriage and offered him a ride; before accepting, however, the man inquired as to which route he was taking and learned it was the new road. Again remembering the old man's advice, he decided to refuse the ride, even though he was near exhaustion. When he arrived in town there was much confusion among the people. Upon inquiry, he learned that the young man who had offered him the ride had been robbed and murdered by bandits.

He began inquiring about his family and learned that his parents were dead and his family were all gone, except his wife. He found out where she lived and then took a room in an inn across the street from her house. The next morning he arose early and began watching the house from his window. In a short while, he saw his wife come to the door with a man and kiss him as he left.

Jealousy rose in him, because even though he had never returned to her, he had always been faithful, and he decided there was one thing he must do before the day ended. He took his gun in hand and sat waiting for the man to return.

As it was nearing dawn, he began to recall the words of the wise old farmer, "Don't shoot at first sight." He then went downstairs and asked the inn clerk about the family who lived across the street. He explained that the woman had been very young when her husband left to seek work. He said that the husband had never returned, nor had he sent support. The woman had been taken in by various families as she was pregnant and in need of help. She remained with these families over a thirty-year period and had worked desperately to rear her son and to educate him for the priesthood.

Just then the same man returned and the husband again saw his wife greet him at the door with affection. He then realized that the man with whom his wife was living was not a lover but a son he had deserted.

# $65.$ Wedding Gift

AN ELDERLY MAN was cutting firewood in a large forest in northern Czechoslovakia. Because it was getting dark and he was alone, he decided to start home, but as he was preparing to leave, he heard men on horseback approaching. Since he knew the woods were infested with robbers, he became frightened. Sending home the horse and cart, which was loaded with wood, he climbed a nearby tree and hid among the leaves.

After a few minutes four men approached carrying two large bushel baskets loaded with money they had stolen.

The robbers stopped directly under the tree where the man was hiding, which was beside a large stone. Under this stone they dug a hole and put the money in it. Then three of the robbers killed one of their friends and left his body on top of the money to guard it. They covered the hole up and put the rock on top of the hole. The money would be safe—until the spirit of the dead robber was saved. This could be done only by having a wedding feast on top of the rock covering his wealth-filled grave. The three robbers then proceeded to leave.

The man in the tree having heard all the conversation, waited until the next morning to be sure the robbers did not return, and then climbed down the tree. He returned home and did not say a word about what he had seen— but he had a plan.

The man's youngest son was sixteen and unmarried. When his father suddenly told him he could marry, the son was overjoyed. However, the father insisted that the

240

wedding feast be held in the woods. Although the son thought this was unusual, he was very much in love with a young girl in their village, and so he agreed.

After the wedding, the couple proceeded to the woods to hold the wedding feast. The man laid the tablecloth on the large rock, and the family began to eat. After the dinner, all were frightened by a voice saying, "You have freed my soul; take the money under the rock."

The man then told of the scene he had witnessed in the woods. After his tale, the men moved the rock and dug up the hoard left by the robbers. The newlyweds, with the money from under the rock, founded one of the richest families in that part of the country.

# *XIII*

# Wise and
# Foolish Folk

## *66.* The Gypsy and the Bear

IN A SMALL CABIN near a wooded section of a small southern European country, there once lived a gypsy. He lived
alone and was content with his way of life, since he owned
a large store of food and did not have to work hard.

One day, while sitting in a chair tilted back against the
cabin and watching the beautiful scenery around him, he
was startled to see a large, vicious-looking bear approaching.
Although very frightened, the gypsy managed to retain
his composure and when the bear was within a few feet

242

of him, asked with a feigned air of annoyance, "What can I do for you, Bear?"

The bear stopped and said, "I'm hungry and I came here to eat you."

The gypsy, a very quick-witted man, replied, "In case you haven't heard, I'm Gregory, the strongest man in Europe, and I can kill you with a single blow. Why not be friends with me, since you are probably the strongest bear in these woods? You can share my cabin and food, and together we will be invincible."

The bear was not completely convinced that Gregory was a stronger individual than himself, but he did not want to take a chance. Living with the gypsy, he would soon find out how strong he really was. So they agreed to live together.

The bear volunteered to cook supper that evening and he handed Gregory a 200-gallon barrel and said, "Take this and get me some water from the well."

The gypsy, knowing he could not lift the barrel even if it were empty, said, "No, we need more water than that. I won't have any use for the barrel."

He then walked out to the well and began to dig a ditch around it. The bear, watching curiously, asked, "What are you doing, Greg?"

"I'm going to move the whole well closer to the cabin, so you can have all the water you need," replied Gregory.

The bear was obviously impressed, but he said. "Never mind; that will take too long."

He then picked up the barrel, filled it with water from the well, and went back to his cooking. The gypsy breathed a sigh of relief.

The next day the bear volunteered to barbecue some

meat outside the cabin and said to the gypsy, "Run over to the woods and get me two or three large trees to build a fire with."

"We'll need more wood than that," said the gypsy. "I'll get all you can use."

The bear watched as the gypsy got a large rope from the cabin and disappeared into the woods. When he failed to return in about twenty minutes the bear went to investigate and found Gregory patiently tying a section of the rope to each trunk of about fifty trees.

"What are you doing?" asked the bear.

"Why, when I have enough trees tied to this rope, I'm going to drag them back to our cabin so that you'll have plenty of wood," replied Gregory.

The bear looked at him with wonder and said to himself, "What a strong man he must be!" But he was impatient for dinner and said, "Never mind; I can't wait." With this he ripped five trees out of the ground and walked back to the cabin with them.

That night, after they had both gone to bed, the bear decided to kill the gypsy while he slept. About midnight, he went outside and got a huge club made from the trunk of a large tree and went back inside to the gypsy's bed and beat the still form under the blankets until he was exhausted. Then he went back to bed and dreamed of the delicious meal he would have in the morning. But, little did he know that Gregory had suspected him of treachery and, when the bear had gone outside, had put old clothes under the covers and hidden himself under the bed. After the bear went back to sleep he got back into bed.

Next morning when the bear awakened, he was shocked to see the gypsy, whistling happily, fixing breakfast.

"Er—how did you sleep last night?" asked the bear.

"Never slept better in my life," replied the gypsy.

"Oh," said the bear, slightly stunned.

Although the bear was greatly impressed by the gypsy's seemingly great strength, he decided to have a showdown. "How would you like to race me to the top of the mountain this morning?" he asked.

The gypsy reluctantly agreed, knowing if the bear won, he would find out that the gypsy was nothing but a bluff and, as a result, would make a meal of him. But there was no way out and so they started up the mountainside, the bear quickly taking the lead with the gypsy close behind. It soon became obvious that the bear would win the race easily.

After several hours the bear reached the top of the mountain and turned around to see how far behind the gypsy was. But Gregory was nowhere in sight.

"What an easy victory that was," thought the bear. "Now, I know I'm going to make a meal of him."

Suddenly the bear heard the gypsy's voice behind him. "Where have you been? I've been waiting for you for an hour," he said.

The bear was so flabbergasted that he ran off mumbling to himself.

The gypsy smiled and recalled how, when the bear began to pull away from him at the beginning of the race, he had reached out and grabbed the bear's tail and hung on while the bear pulled him up the mountainside, and, after reaching the top, how the bear had turned around to see how far he had left the gypsy behind and in so doing had swung the gypsy around behind him, causing the bear to think the gypsy had been there all along.

# 67. The Schemer and the Flute

JOHN AND HIS WIFE dug a hole, put some rocks on it, and covered it with dirt. Then they built a fire on top of the ground. After the fire had burned out, they scraped away all the ashes and made it look like it had before. Then they put a kettle of water on top of the ground; with the hot rocks underneath, the water began to boil. John and his wife sat down and waited.

Two men passed by and seeing water boiling in a kettle, without heat, asked what caused it to boil. John told them that this was a magic kettle. The men looked at each other in amazement. Then one man said, "I will give you a cow for the kettle," thinking how convenient it would be to own the kettle.

John agreed to the trade. He and his wife took the cow home, butchered and skinned it, and put the meat in a smokehouse. While John was taking the intestines away, he thought of another scheme. He told his wife that he would fill the intestine with blood, wrap it around her neck, and that night she was to come to the tavern where he would be, and pretend to quarrel with him. He would then take a knife and cut the bladder as if to kill her, and she would fall to the floor. He would then take out a flute, play it, and she would pretend to return to life. John's wife agreed to this.

That night John went to the tavern. After a while, his wife came and they got into the quarrel, as planned. John pulled out his knife and cut her throat. The blood began to flow freely, and the wife fell to the floor as if dead. The

246

other men looked on in amazement at the brutal murder that had just been committed before their eyes. They asked John what he was going to do. John calmly sat down and began to play the flute. After he had played for about two minutes, his wife got up off the floor, walked outside, down the road, and home.

The men in the tavern were so completely bewildered that they couldn't talk. Finally, after a long silence, they asked John what kind of magic this was. John told them this was a magic flute which could bring the dead back to life. Then he told them that he needed money and would willingly sell the flute, if given the right price. One man thought of all the money he could make by bringing dead people back to life. He bought the flute from John for an enormous sum. John hurried home, packed all his belongings, and he and his wife left town.

In the meantime the man who bought the flute went home. He found his wife with another man and he became furious. The other man ran away, and his wife frantically started to make excuses. He cunningly thought how he would cure her of flirting. He would kill her and, after a while, bring her back to life and really give her a good scare. He took out his knife and cut her throat just as he had seen John do. His wife fell to the floor, dead. After a while he began to play the flute, but nothing happened. Frantically he played; still nothing happened. He tried again and again to play the tune he had heard, but still she remained dead.

He was put in prison for life. And, they say to this day, if you ever go by a certain prison in Yugoslavia, you can still hear someone playing a flute and thinking that the beautiful music could make a dead person sit up and listen.

# 68. The King's Son and the Poor Man's Daughter

THE KING'S SON went hunting, accompanied by a servant, and, when a storm came up, he stopped at a small house. A poor, old man lived there with his wife and daughter. Knowing that the man was the king's son, the family wanted to treat him to the best they had, so they killed their only chicken and had it for supper. The daughter divided the chicken, giving the neck to her father, the backbone to her mother, and the feet to the servant. She kept the wings and breast for herself and gave the two legs to the king's son.

After supper everyone went to bed and the old man and woman discussed their daughter and said, "What kind of a daughter do we have? See what part of the chicken she gave us?"

The king's son overheard them talking, so the next day he asked the daughter why she divided the chicken as she did.

She said, "I gave your servant the feet so he can walk well; I gave Mother the backbone because she is the head of the house and she needs the backbone; I gave Father the neck because one of these days he will have to stretch his neck to see me; and I gave you the legs because you are the king's son and I wanted to give you the best part; and I kept the wings and breast because one day I will fly away from this house.

The king's son thought that she was smart for doing this, and since he liked her very much, he asked her to marry him. She said she would if he didn't mind being

248

married to a poor girl. He said he didn't, so they were married.

Soon after the wedding he told her that she was not to interfere in any of his business, and she said that she wouldn't.

Not long after this, a fair was held near the king's son's palace. One of her poor friends brought a cow to the fair, and, seeing an unused wagon in the field which belonged to the king's son, he tied his cow to it. While she was tied there, the cow had a calf. After the fair was over the poor man started to take his cow and new calf home, but the king's son stopped him and took the calf, saying the wagon had had the calf. The poor man was so afraid that he said nothing. The king's son's wife saw everything and felt sorry for her poor friend, but she remembered that her husband had said she wasn't to interfere in any of his business. She told her poor friend that she could tell him how to get his calf back, but that he was not to say anything to her husband about it.

He was to come back with a fishing hook the next day and go fishing in the field where there was no water, so he did. Her husband saw him and asked what he was doing. The poor man said he was fishing.

The king's son said, "How can you fish here where there is no water or fish?"

The poor man answered him, "How can your wagon have a calf?"

The king's son couldn't answer him and gave the poor man his calf. He knew that the poor man wasn't smart enough to think that out for himself, so he went to his wife. He told her that he'd said she wasn't to interfere in his business, but he knew that she'd thought of the trick, as the poor man wasn't smart enough.

She said, "Yes, I thought of it. Those poor people work hard to raise their cow and calf and they need the money they get from selling them."

Her husband then told her to take all that belonged to her and return home, but that she was to eat supper with him for the last time. While they were eating she added something to his wine, which put him to sleep. She then told the servant to carry him to her home, as she wanted to see her mother and, as her husband was drunk, she didn't want to leave him at home.

While they were in her mother's home, he came to his senses and found himself lying on the floor with his feet in the ashes near the fireplace. He looked around saying, "Where am I?"

She answered, "Right here with me."

He said, "Why did you bring me here?"

She replied, "You told me to take everything that belonged to me, and the only thing I really owned was you, so I brought you here with me."

He then got up and said, "I see you are very smart, so come back with me."

They both went back and lived happily from that time on.

# 69. King Matt and the Wise Old Farmer

KING MATT was a famous king. He liked to go among his subjects incognito, to see how they were getting along. He often said that some of them were smarter than his ministers.

One day he came upon an old farmer plowing his field with his oxen. He asked the farmer, "How far is far, old-timer?"

The farmer answered, "Not very far now; only to the tip of my oxen's horns."

Then King Matt asked, "How many of the thirty-two do you have?"

The farmer answered, "Not so many, sir; only twelve."

King Matt said he had one more question to ask the old farmer. "Could you milk three billy goats?"

The farmer replied, "Yes, sir."

King Matt, at his next court meeting, mentioned this old farmer, adding that he admired his wisdom. He asked his ministers if they understood the riddle, but no one answered. Three of his ministers were so curious that they went and talked to the farmer. When they asked him the answer to the first part of the riddle the farmer said, "I will tell you if you will give me ten pieces of gold."

The ministers agreed.

"Well," said the farmer, "I used to be able to see as far as the horizon, but now I can see only as far as my oxen's horns."

Then they asked the meaning of the second part of the riddle.

"I will tell you for ten more pieces of gold," said the farmer.

The ministers agreed and the farmer said, "I used to have thirty-two teeth, and now I have but twelve."

The ministers then asked the farmer, "How would you milk three old billy goats? After all, they're not milkers."

The farmer said that he would tell them for ten more pieces of gold. After they had given him the gold, he answered, "Milking three billy goats is very easy. I just got through milking three."

The three ministers hung their heads in embarrassment. They never did tell King Matt that they got the answers to the riddle.

# *70.* A Foolish Young Man

A YOUNG MAN named Agor was sent out by his father to sell a wagon full of wheat at the village market. Agor loved to drink whiskey, but he didn't like to pay for it and he never wanted to work. This time he decided he would do as his father asked and sell his wheat.

On his way to the market, he had to pass the orchard of a neighbor, where he saw a gallon of whiskey hanging in a nearby tree. Leaving the wagon of wheat on the path, he proceeded to climb the tree to get the whiskey.

The neighbor saw Agor climbing for the whiskey, so he quietly pushed Agor's wheat wagon into his own barn where the youth could not see it. Agor came down from the tree and realized he didn't have any wheat to sell; in his vexation he dropped the gallon of whiskey and broke it. There he stood with no wheat and also no whiskey to drink—a very foolish young man, who thought he could get something for nothing.

# 71. The Bet

ONE WINTER DAY in Armenia a man named Nasriddin Hoja was talking with some of his friends. The subject they were discussing was whether or not a man could exist in a cave at the top of the big mountain in cold weather. His friends said it was impossible for a man to exist even for one night without any fire to keep him warm.

So Nasriddin Hoja, being an adventurous man, made a bet with his friends. According to the agreement, if he could stay on top of the mountain all night long without any fire or clothing, each of his friends were to give him a brand-new suit of clothes. And, if he could not stay all night, he was to provide them with a big feast.

The next day, in preparation, Nasriddin Hoja took three of his fifty-pound cats to the top of the mountain where he would stay that night. When night came, his friends took his clothes and sent him off to the cave.

Nasriddin Hoja spent a fairly warm night with his cats.

The next morning, when he went to meet his friends, they gave him clothing and said, "You have lost the bet."

"How can you say that?" asked Nasriddin Hoja.

His friends replied, "There was a fire in the next town and that's what kept you from freezing last night."

So Nasriddin Hoja said, "The feast will be on the coming Sunday at twelve o'clock noon."

Sunday arrived and all Nasriddin Hoja's friends were at his house at noon. They waited and waited until finally one of the men got up and said, "Nasriddin Hoja, we have been here for four hours and we are hungry. What has been taking you so long in preparing our feast?"

Nasriddin Hoja said, "It's cooking. If you do not believe me, come and see for yourself."

So they all followed Nasriddin Hoja into the kitchen and saw all the food on a tremendous stove, and in the stove, cooking all the food, was a little candle.

One of the men said, "Nasriddin Hoja, how do you expect this little candle to cook all this food?"

"Well," said Nasriddin Hoja, "if a fire in another town can keep me warm on a mountaintop, then this little candle can cook all this food."

# XIV

# Miscellaneous
# Tales

## 72. The Painted Priests

THERE WAS a couple who lived along the edge of the road,
near a church school. During the day, while the wife
was sitting on the porch, various priests would pass by
her house and would say to her, "Comare, I am dying for
you. I love you."

Finally she told her husband that she wanted to move
away, for she could not stand the place much longer.
Her husband asked her what was the matter, and finally
she told him about the priests.

"So, that is what has been bothering you," he said.

"Well, I'll tell you what to do. Next time a priest says that to you, tell him to come here at night at about eight o'clock when I'm not home, and tell him to bring $300 with him."

The next day as she was sitting outside, Priest Number One came by and said, "Comare, I'm dying for you. I love you."

"Well," she said, "why not come tonight at eight o'clock, since my husband won't be home then? And bring along $300 with you."

"Oh, I'll bring that much and more, if you want me to," he said.

After about half an hour, Priest Number Two came by and said, "Comare, I'm crazy about you. I love you."

"Well, then, come tonight at fifteen minutes after eight, and bring $300 with you. My husband won't see us, for he won't be home."

This continued all afternoon until Priest Number Twelve had gone by. She had told all of them to come that night and bring $300 with them, and each was to come fifteen minutes after the previous one. Of course each of the priests thought he was the only one who was going to see her.

When night came her husband went outside to hide, and she went to bed. At exactly eight o'clock Priest Number One came and knocked on the door. She told him to enter and asked him if he had brought the money. He told her he had, and she told him to put it in the chest that was in the hall. He quickly put the money in the chest and hastened to the bedroom to be with her. When he entered the room, she told him she couldn't stand the smell of the clothes priests wore, so he would have to take them off.

256

No sooner had he undressed, than her husband knocked on the door and shouted, "I forgot my hatchet. Open the door and let me in!"

"Oh," said the wife, "that is my husband. Open the trapdoor and go down in the cellar and wait until he has gone."

He opened the trapdoor, and since it was dark he did not notice that there were no stairs, and fell into the cellar and into a tub of blue paint that her husband had put down there for him.

After a few minutes Priest Number Two arrived. The woman told him much the same thing she had told Priest Number One, and after he had undressed, her husband again knocked on the door and made an excuse for coming back. She told the priest to open the trapdoor and hide there until her husband left, and he, too, fell into the tub of paint.

This went on until all the priests had come and had ended up falling into the tub of paint. After the last priest had fallen into the cellar and paint, the husband nailed the trapdoor shut as well as the outside entrance to the cellar. Then he burned the priest's clothes, and he and his wife sat down to count the money.

In the meantime the priests began to shiver and sneeze, for it was a cold night. Two or three days later the man went to the bishop and told him that he and his wife had been hearing strange noises in their cellar, and that they did not know what was making the sounds.

The bishop came and blessed the house, and then he opened the cellar door. The hungry priests ran out and went home. Never again did they pass the house, saying, "Comare, I'm dying for you. I love you."

# *73.* Pat and the Priest

PAT DIDN'T have a job, so he had to leave home. He had to stay away from his wife, Sophie, for six months. While he was gone, he boarded with a nice family.

When he came home, he went to the priest and confessed he had kissed the landlady goodby.

The priest said, "If you want me to pardon you, you've got to eat a ton of hay. Otherwise. . . ."

When he reached home, Sophie said, "Are you hungry?"

He said, "Yes, but I'll go out to the barn to eat."

Sophie said, "All right. I'll cook."

When she had the meal ready she called, but Pat didn't come. She went out to the barn and found him eating hay.

He said, "I have to eat a ton of hay."

She said, "Tell me why."

He told her he had kissed the landlady, where he boarded, goodby.

She said, "If Father had to eat a ton of hay for every time he kissed me while you were gone, he'd have to eat a lot of hay around here."

# 74. The Monks and the Donkey

ONCE THERE were three monks who traveled in the country and towns, asking the people for food and anything else they could give to the monastery. They were in the country, and after going to all the houses, they were so loaded down that they could not carry all the food home. So when the head monk saw a donkey tied in one of the farmers' fields, he told one of the monks to go and untie it.

The monk said, "What will I do if the farmer finds me?"

The head monk told him to tie himself in place of the donkey, and the two took the donkey and went home. When the farmer came, he was surprised to see the monk there instead of the donkey.

The monk said, "Brother, do not be afraid. Come, untie me, and everything will be all right. I was a big sinner, and God punished me by turning me into a donkey."

The farmer said, "Oh, excuse me for being so mean to you. I didn't mean to beat you and work you so hard."

The monk said, "Oh, that's all right. That was part of my punishment."

So the farmer untied him and he went on his way.

A few days after this there was a fair in that part of the country. The monks took the donkey to the fair to sell him. It so happened that the farmer needed a donkey, and went to the fair to buy one. There he saw and recognized his donkey right away.

So he went up to the donkey's ear and said, "Monk, what did you *do* that you are a donkey again?"

He turned around and hunted for another donkey.

# 75. A Fish Story

OTO WAS a big, strapping man, who was said to be the strongest man in the land. There was nothing that the mighty Oto could not conquer.

One day a traveling man came by Oto's village and told of a great fish in his own country—a fish that no one could catch.

On hearing this, Oto saw a new challenge, and started out for the traveler's country. When he reached the land where the great fish was, he went to the blacksmith's shop and told the blacksmith to get a ship's anchor and sharpen the edges of it. He then went out and bought a cable an inch thick. He returned to the blacksmith's shop and tied the cable to the anchor. For bait, he used two twenty-pound turkeys and placed them on the giant hook.

Oto went to the river where the fish lived. The river was a mile across at this place, and, according to reports, the fish was so large that he needed a mile to turn around in.

Oto grabbed his hook and, with a mighty heave, threw it into the river; not realizing his strength, however, he threw too hard, and it landed on the far bank in a pigpen. Two large pigs saw the turkeys and tried to eat them, but they too were caught on the hook. Oto began pulling in the line for another toss, but while he was pulling the hook across the river, the giant fish grabbed the hook, and the battle was on.

Oto fought the fish for a week without either of them weakening. Finally, waiting until it leaped out of the water, he jumped on its back and began riding it like a horse. The fish bucked like a wild stallion, but it couldn't shake Oto.

The fish, now desperate, gave a mighty leap, and went so high that both it and Oto froze to death. When they landed, the people of the village, with the help of a number of trains, hauled the fish to the north country, so it wouldn't spoil. They put Oto up as a statue in the middle of the square of the new town they built.

The people then took out all the hooks with which unsuccessful fishermen had tried to catch the fish, and there were over a ton of them. Afterward, they removed the scales and sold them for sailboats. On the inside of the fish they built a cannery, and to this day they are canning the meat, and still have more than half of it left.

# 76. The Girl with a Beard

A YOUNG MAN was learning to be a barber. In the old country one had to be a journeyman barber for three years, learning the art of shaving, before he could get his certificate.

In his wanderings the youth went from one barber to another doing odd jobs. When he came to one section, he saw a large castle and hoped they would give him a place to sleep. He saw a watchman, who asked him what he wanted.

He said, "I need sleep. I've been out in the sun all day, and I'm tired out."

The watchman was sympathetic. "You're welcome to stay here," he said. "I've got thirty-five rooms, but I don't think you'll be able to stand it."

"Don't worry. Nothing will bother me. I'll sleep."

He went into one room and everything was very nice, with the table set ready for a meal. He couldn't understand this because the food was hot and there was no one around to eat it. He sat down and waited, but no one came, so he went ahead and ate, thanking the Lord for the food after he had finished.

In the next room, there was a nice bed, so he took off his clothes, said his prayers, and soon fell asleep. In the middle of the night, he awoke and saw a vision above the bed. It was a young woman, who seemed to be in the room, and he thought to himself, "How beautiful you would be if it weren't for your beard. If I shaved you, you'd be as pretty as a picture."

Soon a prince came by on a horse. "What you said, you must do."

The girl sat on a chair while the barber took the soap from his bag and began whipping the lather and stropping his razor. Then he shaved her and said, "Now, see how beautiful you are!"

"I thank you kindly, because I've had this beard for a hundred and fifty years. I was supposed to go to a certain place and select a prince for a husband. I didn't want a husband, but my father told me to pick out a handsome man and get married. I said, "If I take a husband, you must promise to shave.""

He agreed. "All right. I'll shave my beard, but it will grow on your face."

"All this happened just as my father had said. When he shaved his beard for the wedding, it grew on my face. It was a terrible humiliation."

At this time the girl seemed to fade away. Later on, the watchman went on with the story from reports he had heard. The father died about the time of the wedding, and all those who came to the reception left. The princess locked herself in her room, where she remains to this day.

# 77. The Butcher and the Cutter

MANY YEARS AGO in Poland there were two fellows, a butcher and a cutter (an executioner). In those days a butcher had to work three years at his trade and then take an examination before he could be a professional. Similar rules were observed for the executioner. When the butcher had finished three years of apprenticeship, he decided to go to another town. On the way he met a man who asked him his name.

"I'm a butcher."

"I'm a cutter—chop heads off."

"Well, I'm a butcher. I cut heads off too."

Soon they came to a hotel where there was a large group of people eating, drinking, and playing cards. When they stopped for something to eat and the butcher asked for meat, the cutter, who was evidently employed there, brought some.

After eating it, the butcher said, "I never did eat that kind of meat before. I kill cows and everything, but I don't know what this is."

The cutter said, "You don't understand this kind of meat. It's people-meat. This bunch of gangsters here kill people, and I have to slice them up. I kill people too. But tonight, you watch out. It will be the end for both of us. You're a butcher and I'm a cutter, but the gang is going to kill all of us."

The butcher said, "I'm not worried. I've got a dog with me, and he can fight six men, at least."

"That's no help."

When nighttime came, the dog knocked out six of the gang, the cutter did the same for five, and the butcher for three. However, since this was such a large gang of cutthroats, the two men were taken prisoners, and it looked as if it were the end.

The cutter spoke to one of the cutthroats. "Before you kill me, give me one promise."

"What promise?"

"I like to drink wine. All my life I've liked wine. Bring me a glass now."

Each of the two were brought a glass of wine, and their hands freed, so they could drink.

After drinking some wine, the cutter set the glass down and said, "Let all that gang be done away with—make them stiff, so they can't get up any more. This time let your dog do everything. It's too hard for you."

And that's what they did. Then they searched the prisons under the hotel and found a 65-year-old man—a millionaire, who had been a prisoner for many years. Also they found a little girl.

But because there were many gangsters that they hadn't killed, the old man warned the butcher not to lose his dog.

When the cutter had finished his wine, he turned the glass upside down. Later he told the butcher to turn it right side up. He talked to the old millionaire, found he had been a prisoner for seven years, and had not been kindly treated. He decided that he should get the old man and little girl out of there, so he sent them to his home. He then told the butcher to set fire to everything, and burn the hotel and all the outlaws in it, which he did.

The millionaire took the child home with him to live and grow up. The butcher and the cutter both escaped with their lives—and, evidently, the dog too—and went on to have more adventures.

# 78. "El Rabo"

ONE OF the favorite legends told by the people of Compiello, a small village near the Bay of Biscay in Spain, is the tale of a little dog called "El Rabo." This little female dog was so called because she was so small and had such an unusually long tail. "El Rabo" had been around Compiello for years and years. It wasn't the same dog, but the legend has it that "El Rabo" died after she had one litter of pups. Only one dog in the litter looked like its mother, and it was also a female. Therefore it inherited the name of "El Rabo." Then it, in turn, died after one litter of pups, one of which was a female, who looked like the mother, and so on.

"El Rabo" belonged to no one in particular. She would stay around one home for a while and then move on to another. The strange thing about "El Rabo" was that when she chose a home to live in, she seemed to affect the lives of those who lived in that particular place. If the man and wife were not getting along well, there would soon be a change and the couple would be happy and contented with each other. If there were sickness in the home which she chose, good health would soon return. If the family was in financial need, the presence of "El Rabo" would work magic, and things would change for the better. "El Rabo" soon became a symbol of happiness, health, and prosperity.

When she was seen roaming through the village, everyone tried to coax her into coming home with him. The little dog, however, followed none of the coaxers. It seemed as if she knew just the very house where she was was needed and went directly to it.

It is said that there had been an "El Rabo" for more than seventy-five years. The last "El Rabo" had gone to a home where there was much illness and poverty. After the arrival of the little dog, things began to change. The children's health began to improve, and the father, after many months of idleness, found employment.

It is said that a very selfish man came to the home one night and put "El Rabo" in a sack, intending to take her to his house so he would have good luck. "El Rabo" managed to escape and, on her way back to the home from which she had been stolen, got her leg caught in a fox trap. The next morning her body was found by a farmer. As a result of her death, there was never another "El Rabo," but her name will always be a legend in the town of Compiello.

# *79.* "La Bruja"

ONE DAY the priest of the little village of Balboniel in the province of Asturias heard a knock at his door. Opening it he found a thin, white-haired woman who was probably in her late sixties. Her face was so bony that it was actually repulsive. The priest asked what he could do for her. She told him she had lived in many villages, but she had been put out of each because the people called her a witch and feared her. She said she was getting old and wanted only a place to live where she could have a garden and a few chickens and could be left alone to live out her remaining years in peace.

The priest offered her a house on a small farm at the edge of town which belonged to the parish. He said it had a small barn, a good well, and several apple trees. He assured her she could stay there as long as she wished. He also said he would give her a few chickens, some corn, and some seeds for her garden. The old woman knelt and kissed his shoes in gratitude. He took her in his wagon to the farm and gave her bread, eggs, cheese, and milk.

The old woman worked hard planting her garden, tending the chickens, and loosening the soil around the apple trees. She kept away from the townspeople, but eventually had to go into town to sell or trade her eggs for food until she could use the vegetables from her garden.

When the townpeople saw her, they were shocked at her bony face. Most of them would lower their eyes.

Some of them had heard that she had been driven out of the next village, and they complained to the priest. The priest, however, said that the farm belonged to the parish and that the old woman was harmless and would remain on the farm as long as she wished.

Although she was repulsive to the adults, she seemed to have a fascination for the small children. Little by little they began to go to her house. She delighted them with stories and always gave them an apple from the trees which were now bearing large, juicy fruit. The parents cautioned the children to stay away from her, but they seemed drawn to her home.

One day a boy and his sister came to see her and asked her to tell them stories. She did, and then gave each of them an apple, pointing out that since it was beginning to get dark, they should go home. The boy said they would cut through the farmyards instead of going by way of the road, and would get home before dark. They had gone only a few steps when the Bruja called and said, "You must go by way of the road; you must not go through the farmyards."

The boy agreed, but told his sister they would have to take the shortcut, or it would be dark before they got home and their parents would punish them. The girl reminded him that the Bruja had just told them to take the road home, but her brother insisted on going the other way.

When they were walking through the farm of Señor Velaz, the boy was attacked by a dog. He yelled at his sister to run. Señor Velaz heard the children's screams and rushed out and grabbed the dog, which had broken loose from his chain. The boy was saved from severe bites and serious injury by the thickness of his clothing and the intervention of the man. When the parents were told of the Bruja's warning to take the road home, they were grateful for her advice.

On another occasion, little Maria Fernandez was enchanted by a pair of earrings which her mother prized highly. They had belonged to the child's great-grandmother, and although the mother permitted her to look at them, she made her promise never to take them out of the house, since they were a valued heirloom. She told Maria the earrings would be hers when she was eighteen years old.

One day Maria put on the earrings, and her little girlfriend called for her to come over and play. Maria forgot about having the earrings on and went down the road to her playmate's house. When she came home, her mother saw her and said, "What are you doing with that earring on? Where is the other one?"

Maria touched her ears and realized that one was missing. She and her mother retraced her steps and searched and searched for the lost earring, but were unable to find it. As a punishment, the child was confined to the house for a week.

The first day that she was allowed to leave the house, Maria went to visit the Bruja. She told her about the earring she had lost, and that her mother felt bad about it. La Bruja told her to keep looking, and perhaps she would find it yet. She told her to look carefully. She gave the child an apple and told her to sit down, and she would tell her some stories.

She was in the middle of a story when she jumped up suddenly and said, "Maria, you must go home right now. When you reach the spot where the road narrows near the old water pump, you must walk near the edge of the

271

road along the ditch and keep your eyes on the ground."

Maria wanted to know why, but the old woman said, "You must not ask why; just do as I tell you." The little girl promised that she would.

When she reached the spot the Bruja had mentioned, she kept her eyes on the ground. By the side of the old water pump, Maria saw something glistening in the sun. She looked closely and saw it was the lost earring. She picked it up and ran home to show her mother. She also told her the instructions the Bruja had given her.

On another occasion, Ramon, a crippled boy, had come to visit the old woman. After he had been there a while, he said he must go, in order to get a ride on his neighbor's wagon as he came home from work. The Bruja told him he must walk home and not ride in the wagon. At first, Ramon insisted he wanted to ride, as it was difficult for him to walk with his lame leg, but the old woman was so insistent that he walk, that he promised he would not ride in the wagon.

That night at the supper table, he heard his parents talking about their neighbor's accident. It seemed that the horse pulling the wagon was frightened by a large snake crossing the road, and the man could not control it. The wagon hit a large boulder and overturned, and the man was hurt seriously. Ramon told his parents of his intention to ride on the wagon and of the Bruja's insistence that he walk home.

The townspeople still feared the Bruja, but all agreed that her strange powers resulted in good deeds. They accepted her living on the parish farm.

When she died, only the priest and the children went to view her body. When the children went home, they all told their parents that the Bruja in death was no longer ugly. They said she looked very pretty.

The parents, out of curiosity, decided to see for themselves. When they viewed her body, they were amazed. Her white hair seemed to have a golden sheen, and her features to have taken on a look of gentleness. Even her mouth seemed to be smiling softly. They all began to think of how many times she had protected their children from harm by her forebodings and warnings. It was not until she was dead that they all agreed she was not a Bruja at all, but a woman who loved and protected children.

When the Bruja was buried, all who could possibly do so, attended the services and brought flowers. It is said that the birds in the cemetery were so numerous and their singing was so loud that it was impossible to hear the words of the priest.

# Information about Some of the Contributors

JOHN NOVAK came to this country from Poland about fifty or sixty years ago, when he was a young man of nineteen. He came to work in the mines, having previously worked two or three years in European mines. From the age of about eight to fifteen, he spent his summers watching the family sheep and cattle along with other children, all supervised by a Mr. Feodor, a former Austrian nobleman under the Emperor Franz Joseph, until he lost his wealth and health through misfortune and famine. Each evening Mr. Feodor told the children stories and must have had an endless stock, since it seems he never repeated a story.

Mr. Novak told twelve tales, the longest of which was about 4,000 words. Some of these tales were told in Polish and translated by his niece, Mrs. Anne Conley, and some in broken English. In every case, Mrs. Conley made suggestions as to the wording.

Mr. Novak came from the Polish section of Silesia, where the Grimm brothers got so many of their tales; however, he never read Grimm. His tales were all learned by oral transmission, as they were told in Polish Silesia and evidently had been told for hundreds of years. Some of them are rather complicated versions of well-known tale types, and others are composites of many types and motifs.

ROCCO PANTALONE came to West Virginia as a youth from Vacri, Chieta, Italy, in July 1906. He worked in the mines from 1906 to 1952, first working in the Watson Mine. From 1921 until his retirement, he also did farmwork (mostly gardening) for himself and was so successful at it that for a time he raised all the vegetables for certain grocery stores in the area. In 1943, the Pantalone family was given an award in gardening, the Certificate of Farm War Service, by the United States secretary of agriculture.

Some people joked about Mr. Pantalone's planting by the moon, but when he had large crops and they had nothing, they decided he knew what he was doing. Mr. Pantalone follows the almanac rather closely in deciding when to plant and when not to plant.

When Mr. Pantalone first told the tales, I set them down in my notebook, but at a second session they were recorded on tape by his daughter, Margaret, and copies given to me. We have some thirty or forty tales on tape, some of which were told by Mrs. Pantalone.

This storytelling has gone on in the Pantalone family for a long time. When the children were small, the family would sit around the fireplace, and the mother and father would tell stories, or sometimes the father would play the accordion. When there was work to do, such as shelling corn, the whole family worked as the stories were being told. However, although both parents knew the stories and told them, the father has always been the chief storyteller.

Joe Catania came to the United States from Sicily in the early 1900s. He came to work in the mines, where he worked until he retired.

In 1949, Violet Forchi, a student in my folk literature class at Fairmont State College, reported a tale which he had told her in Italian and which she had translated into

276

English, "The Ring". (The Magic Ring, Tale Type 560). Later he told five other tales—one of them was really two tales, since it was called "Two Men's Stories"—varying in length from one typed page, "The Dream" (The Poor Brother's Treasure) to twenty-eight typed pages, "The Story of Hedgy". (The Siegfried legend), an Americanized version which he had evidently told his children from the Sicilian version he had heard as a boy.

ALI ISHMAEL came to the United States from Turkey in 1905. He first came to Pennsylvania, where he worked in the mines, but later he settled in Monongah, West Virginia.

When Mr. Ishmael made the recordings for me in 1950, he was eighty-nine years old, according to his statement, and was retired from the mines, a fact that he resented bitterly, since he still felt able to work.

In addition to telling the story of his life, he told five tales, including an interesting version of Tale Type 725, "The Dream.". Although the story was told in broken English, it was so difficult for me to understand him, in parts, that I don't feel I have done complete justice to this rather complicated tale.

FRANK PAZDRIC came to the United States from Austria in 1910, when he was a young man of eighteen. For the first year, he worked in the steel mills at $2.00 a day for a twelve-hour day, after which he got an easier job, working ten hours a day in a factory for $1.85 a day. In 1918 he started to work in the coal mines, where he remained until he retired.

Mr. Pazdric contributed seven tales, through three students. In almost every case I believe he wrote the stories up for the students, since four of these stories were brought to me as he had written them.

Mr. Pazdric left home at the age of seven, when his mother came to America to be a cook for her uncle, who was a Roman Catholic priest, and the children were taken by relatives. She was gone for seven years, and after her return the family was reunited in the old home.

Mr. Pazdric heard these stories told when he was a boy of about eight, and was watching cattle and other stock, along with several other children. He had to go where his master told him to go, but sometimes three or four of the children would get together and tell stories.

The part of Austria from which he came is now Yugo-slavia and has been since 1918.

Arpad R. Puskas, as told by his son, Frank: My father was born three miles from Budapest, Hungary, in 1900. When he was ten years old, his parents decided to move to America. My father didn't mind that, because all his friends were already in America. When the Puskas family landed in the United States, they settled in New Jersey. My father's father, Arpod, found out that there was a lot of money in the making of whiskey, so, in 1912, the whole family moved to the wooded area of West Virginia. Arpod Puskas figured that the mountainous region was a good place to brew his whiskey.

A year later the parents grew homesick for their native country. My father had just started working in the Grant Town coal mines, when his father and mother decided to leave America. He didn't want to go back, but he was only fourteen years old and had to accompany his parents; a year later, however, he decided to return to the country he loved. He didn't particularly like the coal mines, but because it was the only thing he knew how to do, he returned to the Grant Town coal mines.

While he worked in the coal mines, he made money on the side by selling homemade whiskey. When prohibition came into effect, my father knew that there was a lot of money to be made in the brewing of whiskey. Once again he quit the mines, this time to concentrate on making liquor. He and a couple of friends went to New Jersey to sell their brew. They would make it in the hills of West Virginia and transport it to their store in New Jersey. My father said that the state police stopped them one time in Pennsylvania for a spot check. They had about six gallons of whiskey in the car, and the police were closing in on them. When the police checked the car, they found six empty gallon jugs. My father, who was driving, couldn't understand what had happened to the whiskey. He drove about three more miles and the car conked out! The two men in the back seat had emptied the whiskey into the gas tank.

In 1929 my father went to Brooklyn, New York, to get rid of the extra whiskey that he had. While in Brooklyn, he met a 19-year-old Hungarian girl named Josephine Yambro, and a few weeks later they were married. When she found out about his being in the bootlegging business, she said she would leave him if he didn't quit. So he quit bootlegging and went back to the Grant Town coal mines. He wasn't making as much money, but at least it was an honest living—so his wife told him. Today my father is still working in the coal mines and he said that if it wasn't for that sweet little girl from Brooklyn, he would probably still be looking for that easy buck!

OTHER CONTRIBUTORS: Most of the Spanish stories of Sally Alvarez were told to her by her mother, as told by her mother or another close relative or friend. In many cases the tales are supposedly the experiences of relatives or acquaintances, and at least one, "El Caballo con Alas," is a family legend. The grandmother grew up in Spain.

All or almost all the Hungarian tales of John Yokay—and there were eight or ten of them—were told to him by his grandmother, who was eighty-four at the time. Since the grandmother spoke no English, they were told in Hungarian and translated by John.

Of some twelve tales contributed by Marietta Hervatin Boswell, all were told to her by her mother, Mrs. Grace Hervatin. All but two—Austrian and Russian, respectively, and told to Mrs. Hervatin by her husband—were Italian. Since I was unable to get information about Mrs. Hervatin's early life, I am uncertain as to whether she grew up in Italy or the United States.

In many cases, including the Yugoslav tales of Homer Delavich, there would have been no possible way of getting the stories, except through the help of a younger relative, who also served as translator.

# Notes

1. *The Legend of Twardowski* (Polish)

John Novak, Kilarm, 1951, as told in Polish and translated by by his niece, Mrs. Anne Conley, also of Kilarm.

This version has little in common with "The Master Wizard," the tale about the hero Twardowski generally known by the Polish people, except the selling of his soul to the devil, but is rather a combination or amalgamation of many Tale Types and Motifs. Selling the soul to the devil is a variation of the Faust legend, and some scholars believe that Goethe got his basic idea for the character of Faust from the well-known Polish hero of legend. Since this is a long "hero" story, involving most of a man's life, many Tale Types and Motifs would be illustrated. In addition to Faust, other parallels include Bernard; Dégh; Dorson, *American Folklore*, p. 143; Grimm, Tale 206; O'Sullivan, Tale 23; and Ranke, Tale 58.

Types include: 330 III, Deceiving the Devil (Death); 330 IV, Expulsion from Hell and Heaven; 330B, The Devil in the Knapsack Pounded; 475, The Man as a Heater of Hell's Kettles; 756, The Three Green Twigs; 756B, The Devil's Contract; 804B, The Church in Hell; 810, The Snares of the Evil One; 811, Man Promised to Devil Becomes a Priest; 1170-99, Man Sells Soul to Devil.

Motifs include: A751, Man in the moon; E755.2, Souls in hell; G303.6.3.2, Devil comes in a whirlwind; M211, Man sells soul to devil; S242, Child unwittingly promised. For other Motifs, see Motif Index.

2. *The Man Who Sold His Shadow* (Irish)

Dean Sharp, Fairmont, 1954, as told to him by his uncle, who heard it from older relatives who came from Ireland.

The literary story *The Wonderful History of Peter Schlemihl*, by Adelbert von Chamisso, of a man who "unthinkingly bartered his shadow for gold, and so turned himself into an object of superstitious dread," written some 150 years ago, is certainly related to this story, but is not the same.

Types include: 329A*, Man Gives (Sells) His Shadow to the Devil; 580*, The Inexhaustible Purse.

Motifs include: D1451, Inexhaustible purse furnishes money; E743, Soul as Shadow; F1038, Person without a shadow; M211, Man sells soul to devil. Or see Motif Index.

### 3. Patience (Turkish)

A. S. Bavely, Fairmont, 1952, who learned the story as a child while delivering groceries to thirteen Turkish miners who lived together and liked to tell tales. Two Turkish men were with him at the time I recorded the tale.

There seems to be no exact Tale Type of this, as far as I can discern. In many medieval stories, however, treasures (or castles) rise out of the ground.

Motifs include: D1555.3, Magic formula causes silver to hide itself in mountain; F752, Mountain of treasure; G303.3.3, The devil in animal form; G354.1.1, Demon in shape of serpent guards treasure; N553.5, Tabu: fear of threatening animals while treasure is being raised.

### 4. "El Caballo con Alas" (Spanish—"The Horse with Wings")

Sally Alvarez, Spelter, 1966, as told by her mother.

Types include: 813, A Careless Word Summons the Devil; 817*, Devil Leaves at Mention of God's Name.

Motifs include: C12, Devil invoked, appears unexpectedly; D102, Transformation: devil to animal; G303.3.3.1.3, Devil as horse; G303.6.1.2, Devil comes when called upon; G303.16.3.4, Devil made to disappear by making sign of cross. For other Motifs, see Motif Index.

### 5. General Staats and the Devil

Sam Skeens, Ripley, 1966, as told in his community.

Since General Staats was supposedly a general in the Civil War, this may not have been brought over by the European miners. As far as I know, there are no mines in Ripley. Evidently Staats is some form of Prussian name, and this may be an Americanized version of a more recently European-imported tale.

Types include: 1130, Counting Out Pay; and 1170-99, Man Sells Soul to the Devil.

Motifs include: D1454.1.1.1, Devil runs hands through hair,

coins fall; G303.4.8.2.1, Devil holds fire in his hands; G303.6.1.2, Devil comes when called upon.

6. *The White Bird of Death* (Irish)
   Don Dolan, Weston, 1960, as told to him by his father.
   Evidently, a number of Don's tales are family legends. This particular story seems to be an Irish belief, connected with the death or prospective death of children.
   Motifs include: D1855, Time of death postponed; R185, Mortal fights with 'Death.'

7. *The Godmother* (Italian)
   Joseph A. Monell, Fairmont, 1959, as told by his family.
   Parallels: Grimm, Tales 42 and 44; Campbell, p. 815.
   Type: 332, Godfather Death.
   Motifs include: D1724, Magic power from Death; J486, Death preferred above God and Justice; K557, Death cheated by moving bed; Z111, Death personified.

8. *The Devil, Death, and Simon Greene* (Austrian)
   Betty Sikinow, Worthington, 1954, as told to her by Frank Pazdric of Worthington.
   Type 330, The Smith Outwits the Devil.
   Motifs include: K213, Devil pounded in knapsack until he releases man; Q565, Man admitted to neither heaven nor hell; Z111.2, Death magically bound to a tree( in this case, shut up in a wine cask).

9. *Look in Your Own Backyard* (Austrian)
   William Pratt, Barrackville, as told to him by Frank Pazdric of Worthington.
   Type: 899, Alcestis.
   Motifs include: T11.1, Wife sacrifices self; D1855.2, Death postponed if substitute can be found.

10. *The Curse of the Vampire* (Romania; Transylvanian Alps)
    Anthony Booth, Clarksburg, 1963, as told to him as a child, by his uncle by marriage, Robert Capak, formerly of Bucharest, Romania.
    Anthony Booth wrote this information as a kind of explanation of the background of his Romanian tales.

"Although Transylvania has had its ups and downs, it has been a hotbed for many tales and legends. In these tales I have included a few of my uncle's favorites.

"Some years ago, my Aunt Avis, my mother's sister, married into a family of Romanian stock. The man who became her husband was Robert Capak. Since I was his oldest and favorite nephew, he used to take me upon his knee and tell me stories of his ancestors, some of whom lived in the region of Transylvania. I have retold some of his tales here."

Parallels: Bram Stoker's *Dracula*; Coleman, pp. 123, 125, 129, 144, and 147.

Motifs include: E251, Vampire; E251.1, Vampire's power overcome; E251.3, Deeds of vampires; E251.3.3, Vampire sucks blood.

11. *Footprints in the Snow* (Hungarian)
Frank Puskas, Grant Town, 1959, as told to him by his father.
Motif: E251, Vampire.

12. *Old Man Devaule* (Italian)
Sharon Menear, Worthington, 1965, as told to her by a neighbor who came from Italy. It is supposedly a legend in the family.
Motif: E251, Vampire.

13. *Ivan* (Hungarian)
John Yokay, Carolina, 1959, as told to him by his grandmother.
Motifs include: D113.1.1, Werewolf; D113.1, Transformation: man to wolf.

14. *The Lady Was a Werewolf* (Romanian)
Anthony Booth, Clarksburg, 1963, as told by his uncle, Robert Capak.
Motif: D113.1.1, Werewolf.

15. *The Werewolf of Campobello* (Italian; Sicily)
Tim Slamick, Fairmont, 1965, as told to him by his mother. This is said to be a true happening.
Motif: D113.1.1, Werewolf.

16. *The White Wolf* (Hungarian)
Adella Takacs, Fairview, 1967, as told to her by her grand-mother.
Motif: D113.1.1, Werewolf.

17. *Ears Can Give You Away* (English-Italian)
Rosina Zangari, Norton, 1965, as told in her family.
Motif: D113.1.1, Werewolf.

18. *The Secret* (Italian)
Dave Cimino, Fairmont, 1965, as told in his family.
Motif: D113.1.1, Werewolf.

19. *Fatal Shortcut* (Hungarian)
Frank Puskas, Grant Town, 1959, as told to him by his father.

20. *Seven Bones* (Czechoslovakian)
Anna Krajnak, Fairmont, 1948, as told to her by her mother.
Anna thought it had actually occurred in Czechoslovakia.
The best artistic treatment of this tale is the cantata *The Spectre's Bride* by Anton Dvorak. Also Dégh includes two varia-tions of this, Tales 4 and 69, as does Coleman, p. 21.
Type: 365, The Dead Bridegroom Carries off his Bride (Lenore).
Motifs include: E215, The Dead Rider (Lenore); E266, Dead carry off living; E434.8, Ghost cannot pass cross or prayer book; E452, Ghost laid at cockcrow.

21. *Seven Devils* (Hungarian)
George Lomas, Grant Town, 1960, as told to him by an elderly Hungarian woman.
Parallels: Briggs and Tongue, Tale 23, and Dorson, *Jonathan Draws the Long Bow*, pp. 33-35, are similar examples of dis-gruntled witches who avenge themselves.

22. *Javo's Curse* (Yugoslavian)
Homer Delavich, Monongah, 1957, as told to him by his grandfather.
Motifs include: M341.1.1, Prophecy: death on wedding day; Q556, Curse as punishment; Z111, Death personified.

23. *The Story of Hedgy* (Italian)
Joe Catania, Monongah, 1948, as told in Italian and translated by Violet Forchi.

This is a version of the *Nibelungenlied*, a Middle High German epic poem by an unknown author, written in the early part of the thirteenth century. Wagner's ring cycle of operas, *Der Ring des Nibelungen*, is based chiefly on Norse variants of these legends. Also, there is an old German silent movie, *Siegfried*.

Types include a combination of 300, The Dragon-Slayer; 519, The Strong Woman as Bride; 650\*\*, The Strong Youth; and 650C, The Youth Who Bathed Himself in the Blood of a Dragon.

Motifs include: B11, Dragon; B172, Magic bird; B211.3, Speaking bird; D1361, Magic object renders invisible; D1846.4, Invulnerability through bathing in dragon's blood; T611.7, Abandoned child saved by seagulls; milk furnished by doe. For other Motifs, see Motif Index.

24. *The Bad Boy Who Became a Knight* (Polish)
John Novak, Kilarm, 1952.
Type 300, The Dragon-Slayer, II, III, IV.
Motifs include: B11.10, Sacrifice of human being to dragon; B11.2.3.1, Seven-headed dragon; B11.5.5, Self-returning dragon's heads; B11.11.4, Dragon fight to free princess; L100, Unpromising hero; P412.1, Shepherd as hero.

25. *The Two Brothers* (Hungarian)
Margaret Fleming, Rivesville, 1950, as told to her by an elderly man from Budapest.
Parallels: Ranke, Tale 29.
Types include: 300, The Dragon-Slayer, II, IV; 303, II, The Life Tokens.
Motifs include: B11.7.1, Dragon controls water-supply; D812.6, Magic object received from witch or wizard; E761.1.3, Life-token: track fills with blood; N772, Parting at crossroads.

26. *John and the Giants* (Italian)
Rocco Pantalone, Fairmont, 1960.
Parallels: Cf. *The Jack Tales* by Richard Chase and "The

Gypsy and the Bear," tale 66, of this collection. This is the only Italian Jack tale I know about.

Types include: 314A, The Shepherd and the Three Giants; 1062, Throwing the Stone; 1063A, Throwing Contest: Trickster Shouts; 1088, Eating Contest; 1115, Attempted Murder.

Motifs include: G500, Ogre defeated; K18.1, Throwing contest: trickster shouts; K18.3, Throwing contest: bird substituted for stone; K81, Deceptive eating contest.

27. *Smart Mrs. McCool* (English?)
Faith Brand, Shinnston, as told to her by her grandfather Claude U. Barker, who was born in Barbour County and brought up in Barbour and Harrison counties.
Motif: J1112.3, Clever wife advises husband how to succeed on adventures.

28. *Lucky and the Giant* (English)
Faith Brand, Shinnston, as told to her by her grandfather Claude U. Barker.
Motif: H961, Tasks performed by cleverness.

29. *Mosquitoes* (Hungarian)
John Yokay, Carolina, 1959, as told to him by his grandmother.
Motifs include: A2000, Creation of insects; A2001, Insects from body of slain monster.

30. *The Ring* (Italian; Sicily)
Violet Forchi, Fairmont, 1948, as told to her by Joe Catania of Monongah and translated from Italian to English by her.
Parallels: Cf. Hoogasian-Villa, Tale 20.
Type: 560, The Magic Ring.
Motifs include: D810, Magic object as gift; D860, Loss of magic object; D882.1.1, Stolen magic object stolen back by helpful cat and dog. For other Motifs, see Motif Index.

31. *The Three Brothers* (Polish)
John Novak, Kilarm, 1953.
Parallels: Ranke, Tale 35.
Type: 530, The Princess on the Glass Mountain.

Motifs include: B184.1, Magic horse; D815.2, Magic object from father; H1462, Vigil for dead father; L161, Lowly hero marries princess. For other Motifs, see Motif Index.

32. *The Bewitched Princess* (Polish)
John Novak, Kilarm, 1952.
Parallels: Marie Campbell in *Tales from the Cloud Walking Country* has a version of this, or a similar story with variations, "The Snake Princess," p. 151.
Type: Variation of Type 433, The Prince as Serpent.
Motifs include: D191, Transformation: man to serpent; D721.3, Disenchantment by destroying skin. (This tale seems *not* to be related to Type 507C, The Serpent Maiden, or Lamia.)

33. *The Girl with No Hands* (Polish)
John Novak, Kilarm, 1952, with some suggestions by Anne Conley.
Parallels: Campbell, p. 163; Dégh mentions this tale in her introduction; Grimm, Tale 31; Ranke, Tale 36; Seki, Tale 30.
Type: 706, The Maiden Without Hands.
Motifs include: K2117, Calumniated wife: substituted letter (falsified message); N711.3, Hero finds maiden in (magic) garden; S51, Cruel mother-in-law; S322.1.2, Father casts daughter forth when she will not marry him.

34. *The Switch, the Tablecloth, and the Harmonica* (Italian)
Rocco Pantalone, Fairmont, 1960.
Parallels: Roberts, *South from Hell-fer-Sartin*, Tale 23; Grimm, Tale 36.
Type: 563, The Table, the Ass, and the Stick.
Motifs include: D1030.1, Food supplied by magic; D1401.1, Magic club (stick) beats person; D1415.2, Magic musical instrument causes person to dance; L161, Lowly hero marries the princess.

35. *The Bell of Justice* (Spanish)
Michael Gonzales, Clarksburg, 1967, who learned it from his older relatives.
Type: 207C, Animals Ring Bell and Demand Justice.
Motif: B271.3, The bell is rung by a serpent.

288

36. *The Dough Prince* (Italian)
Joe De Luca, Fairmont, 1964, as told to him by his mother, who learned it from her mother.

Parallels: Roberts, *South from Hell-fer-Sartin*, Tale 15a; O'Sullivan, Tale 19.

Type: 425, The Search for the Lost Husband, II, III, and IV.

Motifs include: D565.5, Transformation by kiss; D2006.1.4, Forgotten fiancée buys place in husband's bed and reawakens his memory; H1365.4, Quest for vanished husband; N825.3, Old woman helper.

37. *The Three Wishes* (Austrian)
Frank Pazdric, Worthington, 1957; this tale was written up by Mr. Pazdric and sent to me by Richard Garrett.

A version of this tale is found in Grimm, Tale 87; also Ranke includes a version, Tale 56.

Type: 750A, II, IVb, and V, The Wishes.

Motif: J2071, Three foolish wishes.

38. *The Leprechauns* (Irish)
Donald Dolan, Weston, 1960, as told to him by his father.

39. *Peggy O'Leary and the Leprechauns* (Irish)
Donald Dolan, Weston, 1960, as told to him by his father.

This seems *not* to be Type 503, The Gifts of the Little People, and I found no exact parallel to this tale. However, the magic dust brought by the leprechauns seems similar in purpose to the use of Puck's flower in *A Midsummer Night's Dream*—to produce love where there is enmity.

Motifs include: F343.0.1, Fairy offers mortal magic objects; F451.3.3, Dwarf as magician; F451.5.1.20, Dwarfs help in performing task; H1286.2, Fairyland quest for magic object.

40. *Patrick O'Dea and the English* (Irish)
Donald Dolan, Weston, 1960, as told to him by his father.

Motifs include: D1561.2.4, Charm gives invisibility; F451.5.1.20, Dwarfs help in performing task; K531, Escape from battle; N845, Magician as helper.

41. *Don Mike O'Dolan* (Irish)
Don Dolan, Weston, 1960, as told to him by his father.

Motifs include: D1561.2.4, Charm gives invisibility; D1723, Magic power from fairy; H923.1, Wife rescuing husband from supernatural; F451.5.1.20, Dwarfs help in performing task.

42. *Friendship of the Wee People* (Irish)
Ann McConaughey, Cameron, 1969; this is a family legend.
Motif: F200, Fairies.

43. *Eleven Brothers and Eleven Sisters* (Polish)
John Novak, Kilarm, 1952, with some suggestions by Anne Conley.
Types include: 303A, Six Brothers Seek Seven Sisters as Wives; and 513, II, III, The Extraordinary Companions.
Motifs include: D231, Transformation: man to stone; F601, Extraordinary companions; R155.1, Youngest brother rescues his elder brothers; T69.1, 100 brothers seek 100 sisters as wives (seven—seven, fifty—fifty, etc.)

44. *The Ax, the Spade, and the Walnut* (Italian)
Joe De Luca, Fairmont, 1964, as told by his mother, who learned it from her mother.
Parallels: Roberts, *South from Hell-fer-Sartin*, Tale 24.
Type: 577, The King's Tasks.
Motifs include: D950.2, Magic oak tree; D1601.14, Self-chopping ax; D1601.16, Self-digging spade; F715.1.1, River issues from magic nut. For additional Motifs, see Motif Index.

45. *The Golden Duck* (Polish)
John Novak, Kilarm, 1952, with some suggestions on English words by Anne Conley.
Parallels: Campbell, p. 70; Dégh, Tale 5; Grimm, Tale 57.
Types include: 550, The Search for the Golden Bird; 506, The Rescued Princess, I. (Part I is The Grateful Dead Man—but there are *no* conditions here of dividing the winnings.)
Motifs include: B544, Animal rescues captive; H1210.1, Quest assigned by father; E341.1, Dead grateful for having corpse ransomed; K1931.4, Impostors throw hero into pit; Q271.1, Debtor deprived of burial; T66.1, Grateful dead man helps hero win princess; W154.12.3, Ungrateful brothers plot against rescuer. For additional Motifs, see Motif Index.

46. *The Boy Who Wouldn't Tell His Dream* (Turkish)
Ali Ishmael, Monongah, 1952. Mr. Ishmael's broken English is extremely hard to understand at times so that there are places in the tape where I am by no means sure exactly what he is saying.
Parallels: Hoogasian-Villa, Tale 16; Seki, Tale 16, in part, at least. Also, Walker and Uysal, Tale 5.
Type: 725, The Dream.
Motifs include: D1812.3.3, Future revealed in dream; H911, Tasks assigned by rival king (or rich man) where boy is hidden; M312.0.1, Dream of future greatness; L161, Lowly hero marries princess (rich girl); M373, Expulsion to avoid fulfillment of prophecy.

47. *The Invited Guest* (Polish)
John Kaznoski, Barrackville, 1961, as told to him by his grandfather.
Parallels: Dégh, Tale 72; Seki, Tale 32, includes Motif D2011. Irving's "Rip Van Winkle" illustrates Motif D2011.
Type: 470, Friends in Life and Death, Parts I and III.
Motifs include: D2011, Years thought days; H1229.1, Quest undertaken by hero to fulfill promises; M253, Friends in life and death.

48. *The Fate of Frank McKenna* (Irish)
Jane McCleary, Clarksburg, 1966, as told in her family.
Motifs include: E366, Return of dead to give counsel; E423.2.2, Revenant as a rabbit (hare); Q556, Curse as punishment.

49. *The Corpse That Wouldn't Stay Buried* (Polish)
Mrs. Anne Conley, Fairmont, 1953, as told to her in Polish by her uncle, John Novak, and translated by her.
Motifs include: E410, The unquiet grave; E459.3, Ghost laid when its wishes are acceded to.

50. *A Visit from the Dead* (Italian)
Judy Prozzillo, Fairmont, 1966, as told in her family.
Parallels: Coleman, pp. 39-42.
Motifs include: E299, Miscellaneous acts of malevolent

ghosts; E323, Dead mother's friendly return; E323.2, Dead
mother returns to aid persecuted children.

51. *King Neptune's Diamonds* (Austrian)
Frank Pazdric, Worthington, 1957. This tale was written up
by Mr. Pazdric and sent to me.
Types include: 1678, The Boy Who Had Never Seen a
Woman; 650**, The Strong Youth.
Motifs include: F639.4, Strong man overcomes giant; L161,
Lowly hero wins princess; T371, The boy who had never seen
a woman. (Actually, it is King Neptune the strong youth over-
comes, and a rich man's daughter rather than a princess that
he wins.)

52. *The Three Godfathers* (Italian)
Rocco Pantalone, Fairmont, 1960.
Type: This is a variation of Type 834, The Poor Brother's
Treasure; or Type 834A, The Pot of Gold and the Pot of
Scorpions.
Motif: N182, Snakes turn to gold.

53. *Blind Wolf* (Turkish)
Ali Ishmael, Monongah, 1952.
Parallels: Seki includes a version of this (Tale 44).
Type: 834A, The Pot of Gold and the Pot of Scorpions.
Motif: N182, Snakes turn to gold.

54. *The Fortuneteller* (Italian)
Joseph A. Monell, Fairmont, 1960, as told in his family.
Parallels: Dorson, *American Folklore*, p. 187; Grimm, Tale
98; Ranke, Tale 54.
Type: 1641, Dr. Know-All.
Motif: K1956, Sham wise man.

55. *The Dream* (Italian)
Joe Catania, Monongah, 1948, and translated from the Italian
by Violet Forchi.
Parallels: Ranke, Tale 37.
Type: 834, The Poor Brother's Treasure.
Motif: N543, Certain person to find treasure.

56. *Christ and the Blacksmith* (Italian)
Rocco Pantalone, Fairmont, 1960.
Parallels: Grimm, Tale 147; Briggs and Tongue, Tale 36.
Type: 753, Christ and the Smith.
Motifs include: K1811, God (saints) in disguise visit mortals; D1886, Rejuvenation by burning; F663.0.1, Smith calls himself master of all masters; J2411.1, Imitation of magic rejuvenation unsuccessful.

57. *The Boy Who Made a Trip to Hell* (Austrian)
Frank Pazdric, Worthington, wrote this story out on wrapping paper and sent it to me, rolled up like a windowshade, in 1957 by Richard Garrett.
Types include: 756, The Three Green Twigs; 756B, The Devil's Contract; 756, The Greater Sinner.
Motifs include: F81.2, Journey to hell to recover devil's contract; Q521.1, Doing penance till green leaves grow on a dry branch; Q545, Murderer's penance complete when he kills a greater murderer and prevents a crime; S211, Child sold (promised) to devil. For other Motifs, see Motif Index.

58. *He Walked on Earth* (Czechoslovakian)
Andy Lepock, Grant Town, 1954.
Type: 766*, A Boy Refuses to Give the Angels and God Food; God Commands Death to Take his Life.
Motif: Q286, Uncharitableness punished. Also includes Motif K1811, God (saints) in disguise visit mortals.

59. *The Beggar's Bread* (Italian)
Marietta Hervatin, Rivesville, 1952, as told to her by her mother, Grace Hervatin.
Type: 837, How the Wicked Lord Was Punished.
Motif: N322.1, Man accidently fed bread which his father had poisoned.

60. *The King's Unhappy Son* (Italian)
Joe A. Monell, Fairmont, 1959, as told in his family.
Type: 844, The Luck-bringing Shirt.
Motif: N135.3, The luck-bringing shirt.

61. *The Snow Boy* (Polish)
John Kaznoski, Barrackville, 1961, as told to him by his grandfather.

Type: 1362, The Snow-Child (variation, since this story is a magical happening rather than a joke).

Probably Motif T546, Birth from water (snow), is better for "The Snow Boy" than Motif J1532.1, The Snow Child, since the boy seems to have miracle traits. (John's "Snow Boy" seems not to be a joke, but more of a kind of miracle.)

62. *The Spendthrift Son* (Italian)
Marietta Hervatin, Rivesville, 1952, as told to her by her mother.

Parallels: Shakespeare's *Timon of Athens* tells much the same tale about the too-generous spender. Also Noy, Tale 14.

Type: 910D, The Treasure of the Hanging Man.

Motifs include: J21.15, Dying man tells son to hang himself if he ever loses his money; N5451, Man in despair preparing to hang himself finds treasure in tree (beam).

63. *The Rooster* (Italian)
Marietta Hervatin, Rivesville, 1952, as told to her by her mother.

Parallels: Hoogasian-Villa, Tale 78; Ranke, Tale 44.

Type: 670, The Animal Languages.

Motifs include: B216, Knowledge of animal languages; C425, Tabu: revealing knowledge of animal languages; T252.2, Cock shows browbeaten husband how to rule his wife; T253.1, Nagging wife drives husband to prepare for suicide.

64. *A Long Wait* (Italian)
Sam Geso, Fairmont, 1965, as told by his grandmother.

Parallels: Roberts, *South from Hell-fer-Sartin*, Tale 32.

Type: 910B, The Servant's Good Counsel (variation).

Motifs include: J21.2, "Do not act when angry"; J21.5, "Do not leave the (old) highway"; J21.6, "Do not ask questions about extraordinary things"; Q491.5, Skull used as drinking cup.

65. *Wedding Gift* (Czechoslovakian)
Diana Evanto, Shinnston, 1966, as told in her family.

Type: 1653, The Robbers under the Tree (variation).

Motifs include: K2296.1, Treacherous robber partner(s) (variation); N595, Helper in hiding treasure killed in order that nobody may find it; N511.1.9, Treasure buried under tree; V67.3, Treasure buried with the dead.

66. *The Gypsy and the Bear* (Russian)
Valentino Zabolotny, Grant Town, 1954, as told to him by his father.
Parallels: Compare with Richard Chase's *The Jack Tales* and "John and the Giants" in this collection. See also Grimm, Tale 20.
Types include: 1030-59, Partnership of the Man and the Ogre; 1049, The Heavy Ax; 1074, Race Won by Deception; 1115, Attempts to Murder the Hero.

67. *The Schemer and the Flute* (Yugoslavian)
Homer Delavich, Monongah, 1957, as told to him by his grandfather.
Type: 1542, The Clever Boy, III, Pseudo-Magic Objects, and IV, Sham Murder.
Motifs include: K112.1, Self-cooking kettle; K113, Pseudo-magic resuscitating object sold; J2401, Fatal imitation.

68. *The King's Son and the Poor Man's Daughter* (Italian)
Marietta Hervatin, Rivesville, 1952, as told to her by her mother.
Parallels: Campbell, p. 198; Grimm, Tale 94; Ranke, Tale 87.
Types include: 875, The Clever Peasant Girl; 1533, The Wise Carving of the Fowl.
Motifs include: H601, The wise carving of the fowl; J1111.4, Clever peasant daughter; J1191.1, Reductio ad absurdum, the decision about the colt (calf); J1545.4, The exiled wife's dearest possession; L162, Lowly heroine marries prince.

69. *King Matt and the Wise Old Farmer* (Hungarian)
Raymond Kalozy, Fairmont, 1955, as told to him by his grandmother, who came from Hungary.
Parallels: Grimm, Tale 152; Child, No. 45, "King John and the Bishop" (variation).
Types include: 922, The Shepherd (Farmer) Substituting for the Priest Answers the King's Questions (variation).

Motifs include: F645.1, Wise man answers all questions; J1593, Any boon desired (variation); H561.6.1, King and peasant: the plucked fowl.

70.  A *Foolish Young Man* (Russian)
Marietta Hervatin, Rivesville, 1952, as told to her by her mother, who learned it from her husband.
Type: 1690, The Fool Gets Everything Backward and Loses Everything.
Motif: J2661, Bungling fool has succession of accidents.

71.  *The Bet* (Armenian)
Contributed by a student, as told to her by her fiancé, who was an Armenian.
Parallels: Similar to Walker and Uysal, Tale 9.
Motif: J1191.1, Reductio ad absurdum.

72.  *The Painted Priests* (Italian)
Melia Mailo, Shinnston, 1957, as told to her by her mother.
Parallels: Walker and Uysal, Tale 3 (variation).
Type: 1750, The Entrapped Suitors.
Motifs include: K1218.1, The entrapped suitors; K1218.1.2, The entrapped suitors: the chaste wife has them caught.

73.  *Pat and the Priest* (Italian)
Rocco Pantalone, Fairmont, 1960.
Motif: X459, Jokes on parsons—miscellaneous. This is really an anecdote about a priest who has done more misdeeds than the man who confessed.

74.  *The Monks and the Donkey* (Austrian)
Marietta Hervatin, Rivesville, 1952, as told to her by her mother, who learned it from her husband.
Type: 1529, Thief Claims to Have Been Transformed into a Horse (variation).
Motif: K403, Thief claims to have been transformed into an ass.

75.  A *Fish Story* (Hungarian)
John Yokay, Carolina, 1959, as told to him in Hungarian by his grandmother.

Type: 1960B, The Great Fish.
Motif: X1301, Lie: the great fish.

76. *The Girl with a Beard* (Polish)
John Novak, Kilarm, as told in Polish and translated into English by Roman Gregory, the father of one of my students.
Parallels: Coleman, p. 49.
Motifs include: D435.21, Picture comes to life; F545.1.5. Bearded woman; M41.1.1.3, Death upon daughter's marriage; P310.9, Magic knowledge of another's thoughts; T321.1, Maid given beard (variation).

77. *The Butcher and the Cutter* (Polish)
John Novak, Kilarm, 1953.
I found no parallels of this tale anywhere.

78. *"El Rabo"* (Spanish—"The Tail")
Sally Alvarez, Spelter, 1966, as told to her by Aureillia Salines.
Type: 201E*, Dog Does Not Spare His Life to Render Services to Man.

79. *"La Bruja"* (Spanish—"The Witch")
Sally Alvarez, Spelter, 1966, as told to her by her grandmother, Macrina Garcia.
Motifs include: K2123, Innocent woman accused of witchcraft; D1865, Beautification by death.

# Motif Index

## C. TABU

## D. MAGIC

## E. THE DEAD

300

303

# Index of Tale Types

# Bibliography

Aarne, Antti. *The Types of the Folktale: A Classification and Bibliography*. Translated and enlarged by Stith Thompson. 2d rev. Folklore Fellows Communications, vol. 75, no. 184. Helsinki: Suomalainen Tiedeakatemia, 1961.

Beck, Horace P. *The Folklore of Maine*. Philadelphia: J. B. Lippincott, 1957.

Bernhard, Josephine B., trans. *The Master Wizard and Other Polish Tales*. New York: Alfred A. Knopf, 1934.

Botkin, B. A., ed. *A Treasury of American Folklore*. New York: Crown Publishers, 1944.

Briggs, Katharine M., and Ruth L. Tongue. *Folktales of England*. Folktales of the World. Chicago: University of Chicago Press, 1965.

Campbell, Marie. *Tales from the Cloud Walking Country*. Bloomington: Indiana University Press, 1958.

Chamisso, Adelbert von. *The Wonderful History of Peter Schlemihl*. Translated by Theodore Bolton. New York: B. W. Huebsch, 1923.

Chase, Richard. *The Jack Tales*. Boston: Houghton Mifflin Co., 1943.

Child, Francis James. *The English and Scottish Popular Ballads*. 5 vols. Boston: Houghton Mifflin Co., 1883-1898.

Christiansen, Reidar Th. *Folktales of Norway*. Folktales of the World. Chicago: University of Chicago Press, 1964.

Coleman, Marion Moore. *A World Remembered: Tales and Lore of the Polish Land*. Cheshire, Conn.: Cherry Hill Books, 1965.

Dégh, Linda. *Folktales of Hungary*. Translated by Judit Halász. Folktales of the World. Chicago: University of Chicago Press, 1965.

Dorson, Richard. *American Folklore*. The Chicago History of American Civilization. Chicago: University of Chicago Press, 1959.

—————. *Jonathan Draws the Long Bow*. Cambridge: Harvard University Press, 1946.

Grimm, Jakob L. K., and Wilhelm. *Grimm's Fairy Tales*. Translated by Margaret Hunt. New York: Pantheon Books, 1944.

311

Hoogasian-Villa, Susie. *100 Armenian Tales*. Detroit: Wayne State University Press, 1966.

Musick, Ruth Ann. "European Folktales in West Virginia." *Midwest Folklore* 6 (1956): 27-37.

——. *The Telltale Lilac Bush*. Lexington: University of Kentucky Press, 1965.

——. "The Trickster Story in West Virginia." *Midwest Folklore* 10 (1960): 125-32.

Noy, Dov. *Folktales of Israel*. Translated by Gene Baharav. Folktales of the World. Chicago: University of Chicago Press, 1963.

O'Sullivan, Sean. *Folktales of Ireland*. Folktales of the World. Chicago: University of Chicago Press, 1966.

Randolph, Vance. *The Devil's Pretty Daughter*. New York: Columbia University Press, 1955.

——. *Sticks in the Knapsack*. New York: Columbia University Press, 1958.

——. *The Talking Turtle*. New York: Columbia University Press, 1957.

——. *We Always Lie to Strangers*. New York: Columbia University Press, 1951.

——. *Who Blowed Up the Church House?* New York: Columbia University Press, 1952.

Ranke, Kurt. *Folktales of Germany*. Translated by Lotte Baumann. Folktales of the World. Chicago: University of Chicago Press, 1966.

Roberts, Leonard. *South from Hell-fer-Sartin*. Lexington: University of Kentucky Press, 1955.

——. *Up Cutshin and Down Greasy*. Lexington: University of Kentucky Press, 1959.

Seki, Keigo. *Folktales of Japan*. Translated by Robert J. Adams. Folktales of the World. Chicago: University of Chicago Press, 1963.

Thompson, Stith. *The Folktale*. New York: Dryden Press, 1946.

——. *Motif-Index of Folk Literature*. New enl. and rev. ed. 6 vols. Bloomington: Indiana University Press, 1955-1958.

Walker, Warren S., and Ahmet E. Uysal. *Tales Alive in Turkey*. Cambridge: Harvard University Press, 1966.

*West Virginia Folklore* 5 (1955), no. 3 (West Virginia-European ed.) Also 2 (1952), no. 2; 3 (1953), nos. 2 and 3; 8 (1957) no. 1; 11 (1960), no. 1.